ACHIEVE YOUR DREAMS

PROVEN STRATEGIES, INSPIRING STORIES, AND PRACTICAL TOOLS TO TRANSFORM YOUR GOALS INTO REALITY

ALEXANDRA HART

CONTENTS

INTRODUCTION

Welcome to "Goal Setting and Achievement: Your Path to Personal and Professional Success." In the pages ahead, you'll discover the transformative power of setting clear, actionable goals and learn practical methods to achieve them. Whether you're aiming to advance your career, improve your personal life, or pursue a lifelong dream, this book will guide you step-by-step on your journey to success.

Importance of Goals in Life

Goals are the compass that guides our lives, providing direction and purpose. Without goals, it's easy to drift aimlessly, feeling unfulfilled and lacking motivation. Goals give us something to strive for and a sense of accomplishment when achieved. They help us grow, both personally and professionally, by pushing us out of our comfort zones and encouraging us to learn and adapt. Setting and achieving goals is crucial for anyone looking to lead a purposeful and successful life.

Overview of the Book's Structure and Contents

This book is structured to provide you with a comprehensive understanding of goal setting and achievement. We begin by exploring the fundamental concepts and science behind goal setting. Next, we'll delve into various methods and frameworks that can help you set effective goals. In the third part, we'll focus on practical strategies to achieve those goals, including creating action plans, managing time, and overcoming obstacles. Finally, we'll share inspiring success stories of individuals who have achieved remarkable goals, offering valuable insights and lessons from their journeys.

Personal Anecdote

When I first started my career, I had a vague idea of what I wanted to achieve but no clear goals or plans to get there. I was passionate and hardworking, yet I often felt lost and unfulfilled. It wasn't until I discovered the power of goal setting that things began to change. I started by setting small, achievable goals, which gradually built up my confidence and momentum. Over time, I learned to set more ambitious goals and developed strategies to overcome obstacles and stay motivated. This journey taught me invaluable lessons about the importance of having clear goals and the dedication required to achieve them. Now, I'm excited to share these insights with you, hoping they will inspire and empower you to reach your own goals.

Setting Expectations

Throughout this book, you will gain:

- A deep understanding of what goals are and why they matter.

- Insights into various goal-setting frameworks, such as SMART goals, OKRs, and vision boards.

- Practical strategies for creating action plans, managing time, and staying motivated.

- Techniques to overcome common obstacles and challenges.

- Inspirational success stories that demonstrate the power of setting and achieving goals.

Each chapter is designed to provide you with actionable steps and practical advice that you can apply immediately. By the end of this book, you will have the tools and knowledge to set and achieve your personal and professional goals, leading to a more fulfilling and successful life.

Encouragement to Take Actionable Steps

As you embark on this journey, remember that the power to change your life lies within you. Setting goals is the first step, but achieving them requires dedication, perseverance, and a willingness to adapt. Don't be afraid to dream big and set ambitious goals. With the right mindset and tools, you can overcome any obstacle and achieve anything you set your mind to. I encourage you to take the lessons and strategies from this book and apply them to your own life. Start small, stay consistent, and watch as your efforts transform into tangible success.

Thank you for choosing this book as your guide. Let's begin this journey together and unlock the potential within you.

PART 1

Understanding Goals

1

WHAT ARE GOALS?

Definition: Clear Explanation of What Constitutes a Goal

I magine you're planning a road trip. You wouldn't just jump into your car and start driving aimlessly, would you? No, you'd have a destination in mind, a map, and a plan. That's exactly what a goal is – your destination, your map, and your plan for life's journey.

A goal is a specific target you set for yourself, something you aim to achieve. It's not a vague wish or a fleeting desire, but a concrete and actionable objective. Think of it as your personal North Star, guiding you toward your aspirations with clarity and purpose.

Let's break this down further. A goal needs to be:

- **Specific:** It clearly defines what you want to achieve. Vague goals like "I want to be successful" lack direction. Instead, a specific goal could be "I want to get a promotion to a managerial position within the next year."

- **Measurable:** You need to track your progress. If you can't measure it, you can't manage it. A measurable goal could be "I want to save $10,000 in the next 12 months."

- **Achievable:** Your goal should be realistic and attainable. Setting a goal like "I want to become a billionaire in a year" might not be realistic for most people.

- **Relevant:** The goal should matter to you and align with other goals. It should drive you forward and be worth your effort.

- **Time-bound:** Every goal needs a target date, so you have a deadline to focus on and something to work toward.

Difference Between Dreams and Goals

Now, let's talk about dreams versus goals. We all have dreams – those beautiful, inspiring visions of what we want to achieve or who we want to become. Dreams are like the fuel that keeps our fire burning, filling us with hope and excitement. But here's the catch: dreams, on their own, are like clouds in the sky – lovely to look at but intangible and fleeting.

Goals, on the other hand, are the steps we take to turn those dreams into reality. They are specific, measurable, and time-bound. If dreams are the destination, goals are the milestones along the way, marking our progress and keeping us on track.

Dreams:

- Abstract and imaginative

- Inspire and motivate us

- Often lack specific details

- Not time-bound

Goals:

- Specific and measurable

- Actionable and realistic

- Detailed and structured

- Time-bound and deadline-oriented

By turning our dreams into goals, we create a practical pathway to achieve what we desire. It's like turning a beautiful vision into a detailed blueprint – the first step in making it real.

Let me share a personal story. A few years ago, I dreamed of becoming a published author. The dream was vivid and inspiring, but it remained just that – a dream. It wasn't until I set a goal to write 1,000 words every day and finish a manuscript within six months that things started to change. By breaking down my dream into specific, measurable, and time-bound goals, I was able to make consistent progress and eventually achieve my dream of publishing a book.

Types of Goals

Goals come in all shapes and sizes, each serving a different purpose and timeframe. Let's break them down:

Short-Term Goals: Short-term goals are like your daily or weekly to-do list. They can be achieved relatively quickly, usually within a few days to a few months. These goals are your stepping stones, helping you build momentum and confidence.

Examples:

- Completing a one-week fitness challenge

- Reading a book in a month

- Learning a new software program within two weeks

Short-term goals are crucial because they provide quick wins that boost your motivation. For instance, if you set a goal to wake up an hour earlier every day for a week, the immediate benefit of extra time can encourage you to continue setting and achieving new goals.

Medium-Term Goals: These goals take a bit more time and effort, usually spanning several months to a couple of years. Medium-term goals are significant milestones that require sustained focus and dedication.

Examples:

- Earning a professional certification within six months

- Saving money for a down payment on a house over a year

- Developing a new skill or hobby over six months to a year

Medium-term goals bridge the gap between your short-term efforts and long-term aspirations. They often require more detailed planning and consistent effort. For example, earning a certification might involve attending classes, studying regularly, and passing exams.

Long-Term Goals: Long-term goals are your big-picture aspirations. They might take several years to achieve, but they define your larger life ambitions and give you direction and purpose.

Examples:

- Building a successful career in your chosen field

- Achieving financial independence and retiring early

- Writing and publishing a book

Long-term goals are your ultimate destination. They provide a sense of purpose and direction, guiding your decisions and actions over an extended period. For instance, building a successful career might involve setting multiple medium and short-term goals, such as gaining relevant experience, networking, and continuously improving your skills.

Each type of goal plays a vital role in your overall strategy for success. Short-term goals provide immediate rewards and motivation, medium-term goals keep you focused and progressing, and long-term goals ensure you stay committed to your ultimate aspirations.

Importance of Setting Goals

Setting clear, well-defined goals is a powerful practice that can significantly enhance both our personal and professional lives. Let's explore why:

Provides Direction and Focus:

Think of goals as the GPS for your life. They give you a clear direction and help you prioritize your efforts and resources. With well-defined goals, you can avoid distractions and stay on course, making steady progress toward your objectives.

When I first started my business, I set a clear goal: to acquire 100 clients within the first year. This goal gave me a target to aim for and helped me prioritize my daily tasks and decisions. Without this goal, I might have spent too much time on activities that didn't contribute directly to acquiring clients.

Increases Motivation and Drive:

Having specific goals ignites your passion and determination. Goals give you a sense of purpose and urgency, motivating you to take consistent action. It's like having a personal cheerleader in your mind, constantly pushing you forward.

Imagine training for a marathon. The goal of crossing the finish line fuels your daily runs, diet choices, and overall lifestyle. Each training session brings you closer to that goal, keeping you motivated even on tough days.

Enhances Self-Confidence:

As you set and achieve your goals, you build self-confidence and belief in your abilities. Each accomplishment, no matter how small, reinforces your sense of competence and capability, encouraging you to take on more challenging objectives.

Consider the example of learning a new language. Setting and achieving small goals, like learning basic phrases or holding a simple conversation, boosts your confidence and prepares you for more complex language skills.

Promotes Personal and Professional Growth:

Goals push you out of your comfort zone and encourage continuous learning and development. By setting ambitious yet attainable goals, you challenge yourself to grow and improve, both personally and professionally.

For instance, setting a goal to become a public speaker might involve overcoming the fear of speaking in front of an audience, learning effective communication techniques, and practicing regularly. This journey of growth not only improves your speaking skills but also enhances your overall confidence and presence.

Facilitates Better Decision Making:

With clear goals in mind, you can make more informed and strategic decisions. Goals help you evaluate options and choose actions that align with your desired outcomes. This clarity simplifies decision-making and reduces uncertainty.

When faced with a tough decision, you can ask yourself, "Does this align with my goals?" This question can guide you toward choices that support your long-term objectives.

Provides a Sense of Accomplishment:

Achieving your goals brings a profound sense of accomplishment and satisfaction. This sense of achievement boosts your morale and motivates you to set and pursue new goals, creating a positive cycle of continuous progress.

Reflecting on your accomplishments, big or small, can be incredibly motivating. It reminds you of your capabilities and fuels your ambition for future goals.

By setting clear, actionable goals, you can harness these benefits and create a structured path to success. Goals empower you to take control of your life, make purposeful choices, and achieve your full potential.

As we move forward, we'll explore various methods and strategies for setting effective goals. By understanding the different types of goals and the importance of having clear objectives, you'll be well-equipped to embark on your journey toward personal and professional success. Remember, the journey of a thousand miles begins with a single step. Let's take that first step together by setting your goals and turning your dreams into reality.

2

THE SCIENCE BEHIND GOAL SETTING

I n the previous chapter, we explored what goals are and why they matter. Now, let's dive deeper into the science behind goal setting and understand how it impacts our brain, motivation, and overall productivity. This chapter will shed light on the psychological and neurological mechanisms that make goal setting such a powerful tool for personal and professional growth.

Psychological Aspects

How Goal Setting Impacts the Brain

Have you ever noticed how setting a goal can instantly shift your mindset and focus? This isn't just a coincidence. When you set a goal, your brain releases dopamine, a neurotransmitter associated with pleasure, motivation, and reward. Dopamine acts as a motivator, encouraging you to take action and pursue your objectives.

Research by Dr. Edwin Locke and Dr. Gary Latham, pioneers in the field of goal-setting theory, has shown that specific and challenging goals lead to higher performance compared to vague or easy goals. Their studies highlight the importance of goal clarity and difficulty in driving motivation and effort.

Dr. Locke and Dr. Latham's Goal Setting Theory emphasizes five key principles: Clarity, Challenge, Commitment, Feedback, and Task Complexity. Each of these principles plays a vital role in enhancing motivation and performance. For instance, clarity ensures that your goals are specific and understandable, while challenge refers to the level of difficulty, which should be high enough to inspire effort but realistic enough to be attainable.

Motivation and Reward Systems

When you set a goal, your brain's reward system gets activated. This system, primarily involving the mesolimbic pathway, reinforces behaviors that lead to the attainment of the goal. As you make progress, your brain releases more dopamine, creating a positive feedback loop that keeps you motivated.

For example, remember the story of training for a marathon from the previous chapter? Each time you complete a training session, your brain rewards you with a dopamine boost, reinforcing your commitment to the goal. This reward system helps you stay focused and motivated, even when the training gets tough.

The concept of "anticipatory dopamine" is crucial here. Neuroscientist Dr. Wolfram Schultz's research shows that our brains release dopamine not only when we achieve a goal but also in anticipation of achieving it. This means that just thinking about your goal and visualizing your progress can provide a motivational boost, helping you stay engaged and excited about your journey.

Neurological Insights

Brain Structures Involved in Goal Setting

Goal setting involves several key brain structures, including the prefrontal cortex (PFC), the amygdala, and the striatum. The PFC, located at the front of your brain, plays a crucial role in planning, decision-making, and self-control. It helps you formulate your goals, create action plans, and stay disciplined in your efforts.

The amygdala, an almond-shaped structure deep within the brain, is involved in emotional processing. It helps you evaluate the emotional significance of your goals, making them more meaningful and motivating. When you set a goal that resonates emotionally, the amygdala's activation can amplify your commitment and drive.

The striatum, part of the brain's reward system, is responsible for reinforcing goal-directed behaviors. It processes the rewards associated with goal achievement, driving you to continue your efforts.

Dr. Kent Berridge's research on the striatum and the reward system highlights how this brain region integrates both the anticipation and receipt of rewards, making it a central player in sustaining motivation.

Neuroplasticity and Habit Formation

Neuroplasticity is the brain's ability to reorganize itself by forming new neural connections. When you set and pursue goals, you engage in activities that strengthen specific neural pathways, enhancing your ability to achieve similar goals in the future.

For example, let's revisit the goal of learning a new language from the previous chapter. As you practice speaking, listening, and writing in the new language, your brain forms new connections that make these tasks easier over time. This process of habit formation is driven by neuroplasticity, enabling you to develop and refine your skills.

Dr. Carol Dweck's research on growth mindset also emphasizes the role of neuroplasticity in achieving goals. According to her studies, individuals who believe in their ability to grow and improve (growth mindset) are more likely to set challenging goals and persist in their efforts, compared to those with a fixed mindset.

In a study conducted by Dr. Michael Merzenich, a pioneer in neuroplasticity, it was demonstrated that consistent practice and goal-directed behavior can lead to significant changes in brain structure and function. This means that as you work towards your goals, your brain adapts and becomes more efficient at the tasks required to achieve them.

Benefits

Increased Focus and Productivity

One of the most significant benefits of setting goals is the increased focus and productivity it brings. When you have a clear goal, your brain knows what to prioritize, helping you allocate your time and resources more effectively. This heightened focus allows you to work more efficiently and achieve better results.

Consider the example of setting a goal to complete a professional certification within six months. With this goal in mind, you can create a study schedule, prioritize your tasks, and avoid distractions that might derail your progress. This focused approach boosts your productivity and increases your chances of success.

A study by Dr. Gail Matthews, a psychology professor at Dominican University of California, found that individuals who wrote down their goals, shared them with a friend, and sent weekly updates were significantly more likely to achieve their goals compared to those who kept their goals to themselves. This research underscores the importance of goal specificity and accountability in enhancing focus and productivity.

Enhanced Self-Esteem and Confidence

Achieving your goals has a profound impact on your self-esteem and confidence. Each time you accomplish a goal, your brain reinforces the belief in your abilities, boosting your self-efficacy. This increased confidence motivates you to set and pursue even more ambitious goals.

For instance, let's go back to the story of building a successful career. Each promotion or milestone you achieve reinforces your belief in your capabilities, encouraging you to take on new challenges and continue advancing in your career. This positive cycle of goal setting, achievement, and confidence building propels you toward greater success.

A study conducted by Dr. Albert Bandura, a renowned psychologist, highlights the importance of self-efficacy in goal achievement. His research shows that individuals with high self-efficacy are more likely to set challenging goals, persist in their efforts, and achieve their desired outcomes. Bandura's work emphasizes the role of belief in one's abilities as a critical factor in the pursuit and attainment of goals.

Promotes Personal and Professional Growth

Goals push you out of your comfort zone and encourage continuous learning and development. By setting ambitious yet attainable goals, you challenge yourself to grow and improve, both personally and professionally.

For instance, setting a goal to become a public speaker might involve overcoming the fear of speaking in front of an audience, learning effective communication techniques, and practicing regularly. This journey of growth not only improves your speaking skills but also enhances your overall confidence and presence.

Dr. Anders Ericsson's research on deliberate practice underscores the importance of setting specific, challenging goals for skill development. His studies suggest that individuals who engage in deliberate practice, with clear goals and focused efforts, achieve higher levels of performance and expertise compared to those who practice less intentionally.

Facilitates Better Decision Making

With clear goals in mind, you can make more informed and strategic decisions. Goals help you evaluate options and choose actions that align with your desired outcomes. This clarity simplifies decision-making and reduces uncertainty.

When faced with a tough decision, you can ask yourself, "Does this align with my goals?" This question can guide you toward choices that support your long-term objectives.

For example, if you're considering taking on a new project at work, you can assess whether it aligns with your career advancement goals. If the project offers opportunities for skill development and networking that support your goals, it's a strategic choice to pursue it.

Provides a Sense of Accomplishment

Achieving your goals brings a profound sense of accomplishment and satisfaction. This sense of achievement boosts your morale and motivates you to set and pursue new goals, creating a positive cycle of continuous progress.

Reflecting on your accomplishments, big or small, can be incredibly motivating. It reminds you of your capabilities and fuels your ambition for future goals. Celebrating these wins, even through simple acknowledgments, can reinforce your commitment to ongoing growth and success.

A study published in the Journal of Personality and Social Psychology found that individuals who regularly set and achieve goals experience higher levels of well-being and life satisfaction. This research highlights the broader impact of goal achievement on overall happiness and fulfillment.

In this chapter, we've explored the psychological and neurological foundations of goal setting. Understanding how goal setting impacts the brain, motivation, and behavior provides valuable insights into why this practice is so effective. By harnessing the power of your brain's reward system and neuroplasticity, you can set and achieve goals that lead to increased focus, productivity, and confidence.

As we move forward, we'll delve into various methods and strategies for setting effective goals. By applying these scientific principles, you'll be better equipped to embark on your journey toward personal and professional success. Remember, every small step you take brings you closer to your ultimate destination. Let's continue this journey together and unlock the full potential of goal setting.

3

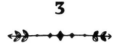

Common Myths About Goal Setting

In the previous chapter, we delved into the science behind goal setting, understanding how our brain supports and enhances our efforts toward achieving our objectives. However, despite the overwhelming evidence supporting the efficacy of goal setting, several myths and misconceptions persist. These myths can deter people from setting goals or lead them astray in their goal-setting journey. In this chapter, we'll dispel these common myths, explore the reasons why some people fail to achieve their goals, and share real-life examples of goal-setting failures and successes.

Dispelling Myths

Common Misconceptions

Myth 1: Goals Are Too Rigid

One of the most prevalent myths is that setting goals makes your life rigid and inflexible. People often think that once they set a goal, they must follow a strict, unchanging path to achieve it. However, this is far from the truth.

Truth: Goals Are Dynamic and Adaptable

Goals provide direction and purpose, but they are not set in stone. They can and should be adjusted as circumstances change. Flexibility is crucial in goal setting. Life is unpredictable, and being able to adapt your goals to new situations is a strength, not a weakness.

For instance, let's consider someone training for a marathon. They might set a goal to run a specific number of miles each week. If they get injured, sticking rigidly to this goal could cause more harm. Instead, they can adapt their training plan to include low-impact activities that maintain their fitness without aggravating the injury.

A study by Dr. John Norcross, a psychology professor at the University of Scranton, found that people who adjust their goals in response to setbacks are more likely to succeed than those who stubbornly stick to their original plans. This adaptability is a key component of successful goal achievement.

Myth 2: Setting Goals Limits Creativity

Another misconception is that setting goals stifles creativity. The belief is that having structured objectives can limit your ability to think outside the box and explore new possibilities.

Truth: Goals Enhance Creativity by Providing Focus

While it might seem counterintuitive, setting goals can actually enhance creativity by providing a clear focus. When you know what you're aiming for, you can channel your creative energies more effectively. Goals help you prioritize your efforts and allocate your resources toward the most impactful activities.

Consider the example of writing a book. Without a goal, an aspiring author might write sporadically and without direction. However, by setting specific goals – such as writing a certain number of words each day – they can establish a consistent writing routine that fosters creativity and productivity. This focused approach allows the author to explore different ideas and themes within the framework of their goal.

Myth 3: Goals Are Only for Big Achievements

Some people believe that goal setting is only necessary for significant, life-changing achievements, such as starting a business or running a marathon. They might think that setting goals for smaller tasks is unnecessary.

Truth: Goals Are Beneficial for All Achievements

Goals are beneficial for both big and small achievements. Setting goals for smaller tasks can build momentum and provide a sense of accomplishment, which in turn boosts motivation for larger goals. Every goal, regardless of its size, contributes to your overall growth and progress.

For example, setting a goal to read a book each month can enhance your knowledge and provide a sense of achievement. This small goal can create a habit of continuous learning, which can support larger career or personal development goals in the long run.

Why Some People Fail

Lack of Planning and Commitment

One of the primary reasons people fail to achieve their goals is a lack of planning and commitment. Setting a goal is just the first step. Without a detailed plan and a commitment to follow through, goals can quickly fall by the wayside.

Planning: The Roadmap to Success

Effective planning involves breaking down your goal into smaller, manageable tasks and setting deadlines for each step. This approach not only makes the goal seem less daunting but also provides a clear roadmap for achieving it. A study by Dr. Gail Matthews found that individuals who wrote down their goals and developed action plans were 33% more likely to achieve their goals compared to those who didn't.

Commitment: The Fuel for Perseverance

Commitment is equally important. It's the determination to stick with your plan, even when faced with obstacles. Commitment requires self-discipline and the ability to stay focused on your goal, despite distractions or setbacks.

External vs. Internal Motivation

Another factor influencing goal achievement is the source of motivation. Motivation can be external (driven by rewards or recognition) or internal (driven by personal satisfaction and intrinsic values).

External Motivation:

External motivation, such as receiving a promotion or winning a competition, can be powerful but is often short-lived. Once the external reward is achieved, the motivation may wane. For example, an employee might work hard to get a bonus, but after receiving it, their motivation might decrease.

Internal Motivation:

Internal motivation, on the other hand, is more sustainable. It comes from within and is driven by personal values, passion, and satisfaction. When you're internally motivated, the process itself is rewarding, and you're more likely to stay committed to your goals in the long run.

Research by Dr. Edward Deci and Dr. Richard Ryan on Self-Determination Theory highlights the importance of internal motivation. Their studies show that people who are intrinsically motivated are more likely to persist in their efforts and achieve their goals, as their motivation is aligned with their core values and interests.

Case Studies

Real-Life Examples of Goal-Setting Failures and Successes

To understand the dynamics of goal setting better, let's explore some real-life examples of both failures and successes.

Failure Case Study: Overlooking the Importance of Planning

Consider the story of Jane, an ambitious marketing professional who set a goal to launch her own startup within a year. Excited by her vision, she quit her job and dove into her new venture without a detailed plan. Jane underestimated the importance of market research, financial planning, and networking. Within six months, she ran out of funds and had to close her startup.

Jane's failure highlights the critical role of planning in goal achievement. Despite her passion and commitment, the lack of a solid plan led to her downfall. This example underscores the importance of breaking down goals into actionable steps and preparing for potential challenges.

Success Case Study: Combining Planning with Adaptability

Now, let's look at the story of Alex, who set a goal to complete a triathlon. Unlike Jane, Alex took a meticulous approach. He researched training programs, created a detailed workout schedule, and joined a local triathlon club for support and accountability. Halfway through his training, Alex suffered a knee injury. Instead of giving up, he adapted his plan to include swimming and cycling, focusing on rehabilitation.

Alex's story demonstrates the power of combining planning with adaptability. His commitment to his goal, coupled with the flexibility to adjust his plan, enabled him to stay on track and ultimately complete the triathlon.

Failure Case Study: Relying Solely on External Motivation

Consider the case of Mark, a sales executive who set a goal to become the top salesperson in his company to win a prestigious award. Driven by the external reward, Mark initially worked hard and saw significant results. However, after achieving his goal and receiving the award, his motivation plummeted. Without a deeper, internal drive, he struggled to maintain his performance.

Mark's experience illustrates the limitations of relying solely on external motivation. While external rewards can provide a temporary boost, they often fail to sustain long-term commitment and effort.

Success Case Study: Leveraging Internal Motivation

Finally, let's examine the journey of Lisa, a teacher who set a goal to earn a master's degree in education. Lisa's motivation was deeply internal – she was passionate about improving her teaching skills and making a positive impact on her students. Despite balancing work and family responsibilities, Lisa remained committed to her goal. She found joy in the learning process and continuously sought ways to apply her new knowledge in the classroom.

Lisa's success highlights the enduring power of internal motivation. Her passion and intrinsic drive kept her focused and dedicated, leading to the successful attainment of her goal.

In this chapter, we've debunked common myths about goal setting, explored the reasons why some people fail to achieve their goals, and examined real-life examples of both failures and successes. Understanding these dynamics can help you navigate your own goal-setting journey more effectively. By embracing flexibility, committing to detailed planning, and fostering internal motivation, you can overcome obstacles and achieve your objectives.

As we move forward, we'll delve into various methods and frameworks for setting effective goals. Armed with the knowledge of these common pitfalls and strategies to avoid them, you'll be better equipped to set and achieve meaningful goals that lead to personal and professional growth. Let's continue this journey together, turning potential setbacks into opportunities for success.

PART 2

Methods for Setting Goals

4

THE SMART METHOD

In the previous chapters, we've explored the fundamentals of goal setting, delving into the science behind it, and debunking common myths. Now, it's time to move into the practical aspects of setting goals. One of the most effective and widely-used frameworks for goal setting is the SMART method. This chapter will provide a comprehensive guide to the SMART method, helping you create goals that are clear, actionable, and achievable.

Introduction to SMART

The SMART method is an acronym that stands for Specific, Measurable, Achievable, Relevant, and Time-bound. It is a framework designed to help you set clear and attainable goals by breaking down the goal-setting process into five distinct components.

- **Specific:** Your goal should be clear and specific, otherwise, you won't be able to focus your efforts or feel truly motivated to achieve it. When drafting your goal, try to answer the five "W" questions: What do I want to accomplish? Why is this goal important? Who is involved? Where is it located? Which resources or limits are involved?

- **Measurable:** It's important to have measurable goals, so you can track your progress and stay motivated. Assessing progress helps you to stay focused, meet your deadlines, and feel the excitement of getting closer to achieving your goal. A measurable goal should address questions such as: How much? How many? How will I know when it is accomplished?

- **Achievable:** Your goal also needs to be realistic and attainable to be successful. In other words, it should stretch your abilities but still remain possible. When you set an achievable goal, you may be able to identify previously overlooked opportunities or resources that can bring you closer to it. An achievable goal will usually answer questions like: How can I accomplish this goal? How realistic is the goal, based on other constraints, such as financial factors?

- **Relevant:** This step is about ensuring that your goal matters to you, and that it also aligns with other relevant goals.

We all need support and assistance in achieving our goals, but it's important to retain control over them. So, ensure that your plans drive everyone forward, but that you're still responsible for achieving your own goal. A relevant goal can answer "yes" to these questions: Does this seem worthwhile? Is this the right time? Does this match our other efforts/needs? Am I the right person to reach this goal? Is it applicable in the current socio-economic environment?

- **Time-bound:** Every goal needs a target date, so that you have a deadline to focus on and something to work toward. This part of the SMART goal criteria helps to prevent everyday tasks from taking priority over your longer-term goals. A time-bound goal will usually answer these questions: When? What can I do six months from now? What can I do six weeks from now? What can I do today?

Detailed Breakdown

Specific: How to Define Precise Goals

The first step in setting a SMART goal is to be as specific as possible. Vague goals lead to vague results. Specificity provides clarity and direction, making it easier to understand what you need to do.

For example, instead of saying, "I want to get fit," a specific goal would be, "I want to lose 10 pounds in three months by going to the gym three times a week and following a healthy diet."

Research by Dr. Gail Matthews at the Dominican University of California found that people who wrote down their specific goals were significantly more likely to achieve them compared to those who did not. This specificity helps to create a clear roadmap for your actions.

Measurable: Setting Criteria for Success

A goal must be measurable to track your progress and stay motivated. Measuring progress helps you stay on track and reach your target dates. It also provides a sense of accomplishment as you reach your milestones.

Using the previous example, "I want to lose 10 pounds in three months by going to the gym three times a week and following a healthy diet," the measurable component is losing 10 pounds. You can track your weight loss each week to see how close you are to reaching your goal.

The importance of measurable goals is highlighted in a study by Dr. Robert S. Rubin at Saint Louis University, which emphasizes that measurable goals help individuals to identify precisely when and how their goals can be achieved.

Achievable: Ensuring Goals Are Realistic

Setting an achievable goal means that it should be within your capabilities and resources. It should stretch you slightly so you feel challenged, but well-defined enough that you can actually achieve it.

For instance, if you set a goal to "lose 50 pounds in one month," it's unrealistic and unattainable for most people. Instead, "lose 10 pounds in three months" is an achievable goal. Ensure that you have the tools, skills, and support needed to achieve your goal.

Dr. Edwin Locke's goal-setting theory states that goals that are perceived as challenging but achievable can motivate higher performance. This balance between challenge and attainability is crucial.

Relevant: Aligning Goals with Personal Values

Your goals should align with your broader objectives, values, and other relevant goals. This alignment ensures that your goal matters to you and that you are motivated to achieve it.

Ask yourself why the goal is important to you. For example, "losing 10 pounds in three months" should connect to a broader personal value, such as improving your health or boosting your self-confidence.

A study conducted by the University of Hertfordshire found that people are more likely to achieve their goals when those goals are aligned with their intrinsic values and motivations. This alignment ensures that the goals are personally meaningful.

Time-bound: Setting Deadlines

Every goal needs a deadline to focus your efforts and create a sense of urgency. A time-bound goal helps prevent everyday tasks from overshadowing your longer-term aspirations.

Continuing with our example, "losing 10 pounds in three months" provides a clear timeframe. It allows you to break down the goal into smaller tasks, such as weekly workout sessions and dietary adjustments, ensuring you stay on track.

Research by Dr. Alexander Rozental from Stockholm University highlights that time constraints can significantly boost motivation and productivity, making it easier to achieve your goals within the specified period.

Examples of SMART Goals

To better understand how to apply the SMART method, let's look at examples across different areas:

Health:

- **Specific:** I want to run a 5K race.

- **Measurable:** I will train three days a week for the next 12 weeks.

- **Achievable:** I can realistically commit to this training schedule given my current fitness level.

- **Relevant:** Running a 5K aligns with my goal of improving my overall fitness.

- **Time-bound:** I will sign up for a race that is exactly 12 weeks from now.

Career:

- **Specific:** I want to get a promotion to a managerial position.

- **Measurable:** I will complete the necessary leadership training and take on three new projects in the next six months.

- **Achievable:** I have the support of my supervisor and the opportunity to enroll in the leadership program.

- **Relevant:** This promotion aligns with my long-term career goals.

- **Time-bound:** I aim to achieve this promotion within the next year.

Personal Growth:

- **Specific:** I want to read more books.

- **Measurable:** I will read one book per month.

- **Achievable:** I can dedicate at least 30 minutes each day to reading.

- **Relevant:** Reading more aligns with my goal of lifelong learning.

- **Time-bound:** I will start this goal at the beginning of next month and continue for the next 12 months.

In this chapter, we've explored the SMART method, a powerful framework for setting clear, actionable, and achievable goals. By breaking down your goals into specific, measurable, achievable, relevant, and time-bound components, you create a detailed roadmap for success.

As we move forward, we'll delve into other goal-setting frameworks and techniques, building on the foundational principles of the SMART method. By applying these strategies, you'll be well-equipped to set and achieve meaningful goals that drive personal and professional growth. Remember, the journey toward achieving your goals starts with a single, SMART step. Let's continue this journey together, turning your aspirations into reality.

5

❧❧ · · ✦ · · ❧❧

OTHER GOAL-SETTING FRAMEWORKS

In the previous chapter, we delved into the SMART method, a reliable and widely-used framework for setting and achieving goals. While SMART goals provide a robust foundation, other goal-setting frameworks can offer additional perspectives and strategies. In this chapter, we'll explore three alternative frameworks: OKRs (Objectives and Key Results), BHAGs (Big Hairy Audacious Goals), and WOOP (Wish, Outcome, Obstacle, Plan). These frameworks can complement the SMART method and provide further tools to achieve your aspirations.

Introduction to Other Frameworks

Overview of OKRs, BHAGs, and WOOP

Different situations and goals may require different approaches. While the SMART method is excellent for creating clear and attainable goals, you might find that OKRs help align team efforts, BHAGs push your boundaries, and WOOP helps navigate obstacles. Each of these frameworks offers unique benefits and can be particularly effective when used in combination.

- **OKRs (Objectives and Key Results):** A framework often used in organizations to set and track goals. OKRs help align personal and team objectives with measurable results.

- **BHAGs (Big Hairy Audacious Goals):** A concept that encourages setting ambitious, long-term goals that can inspire and motivate.

- **WOOP (Wish, Outcome, Obstacle, Plan):** A mental contrasting technique that involves envisioning your goals, the outcomes, the obstacles, and planning to overcome them.

OKRs: Objectives and Key Results

Explanation and Benefits

The OKR framework, popularized by companies like Google and Intel, is designed to connect individual goals with the broader objectives of the organization. The core idea is to establish clear objectives (the "what") and define key results (the "how") to measure progress.

How to Set and Measure Objectives and Key Results

1. **Setting Objectives:** Objectives are the clearly defined goals that you want to achieve. They should be ambitious yet attainable, providing a clear direction.

   ○ Example: "Improve overall customer satisfaction."

2. **Defining Key Results:** Key results are specific, measurable outcomes that indicate whether you are making progress toward your objective. Each objective should have 3-5 key results.

   ○ Example: "Increase the Net Promoter Score (NPS) by 10 points within six months."

Benefits of OKRs:

- **Alignment:** Ensures that individual and team efforts align with the organization's strategic goals.

- **Transparency:** Makes goals and progress visible across the organization, fostering a culture of accountability.

- **Focus:** Helps prioritize key initiatives and allocate resources effectively.

A study by John Doerr, a venture capitalist who introduced OKRs to Google, found that organizations using OKRs often achieve higher engagement and performance levels. This framework's structured approach can keep teams focused on the most critical tasks, enhancing overall productivity and success.

BHAGs: Big Hairy Audacious Goals

Concept of Big Hairy Audacious Goals

The term BHAG, coined by Jim Collins and Jerry Porras in their book "Built to Last," refers to long-term, audacious goals that are clear and compelling. BHAGs are meant to challenge and inspire individuals and organizations to strive for extraordinary achievements.

Setting Ambitious, Long-Term Goals

1. **Visionary:** BHAGs should be bold and align with your long-term vision.

   ◦ Example: "Become the leading provider of renewable energy solutions in the world by 2030."

2. **Clear and Compelling:** BHAGs should be easy to grasp and inspire excitement and commitment.

   ◦ Example: "Land a human on Mars and return them

safely to Earth by the end of the decade." (a famous BHAG set by President John F. Kennedy)

3. **Time Frame:** BHAGs typically have a long time horizon, often 10-30 years, allowing for sustained effort and progress.

    ○ Example: "Eradicate extreme poverty globally within 25 years."

Benefits of BHAGs:

- **Inspiration:** Drives individuals and organizations to reach beyond their comfort zones.

- **Focus:** Provides a clear long-term direction that can guide strategic planning and decision-making.

- **Commitment:** Fosters a deep sense of purpose and dedication.

Jim Collins' research suggests that organizations with well-defined BHAGs are more likely to achieve exceptional performance and long-term success. These ambitious goals can create a sense of urgency and purpose, driving innovation and resilience.

WOOP: Wish, Outcome, Obstacle, Plan

Explanation of Wish, Outcome, Obstacle, Plan

WOOP is a mental strategy developed by psychologist Dr. Gabriele Oettingen. It stands for Wish, Outcome, Obstacle, Plan and is designed to help individuals turn their wishes into concrete goals by anticipating and planning for obstacles.

Practical Application in Daily Life

1. **Wish:** Identify a meaningful and challenging goal.

   ○ Example: "I wish to run a marathon."

2. **Outcome:** Visualize the best possible outcome of achieving your wish. This step boosts motivation and clarifies the goal's benefits.

   ○ Example: "Finishing the marathon will make me feel accomplished and improve my fitness."

3. **Obstacle:** Consider the internal and external obstacles that could hinder your progress. This realistic assessment helps prepare for challenges.

   ○ Example: "I might struggle with maintaining a consistent training schedule."

4. **Plan:** Develop a concrete plan to overcome the identified obstacles using the "if-then" format.

   ○ Example: "If I feel too tired to train, then I will do a

shorter workout instead to keep my momentum."

Benefits of WOOP:

- **Realism:** Encourages a balanced perspective by acknowledging potential obstacles and planning for them.

- **Motivation:** Enhances commitment by linking wishes to concrete actions.

- **Flexibility:** Allows for adaptive strategies when faced with challenges.

Studies by Dr. Oettingen and her colleagues have shown that WOOP can significantly increase goal achievement across various domains, including health, academics, and personal development. The WOOP method's emphasis on planning for obstacles helps individuals remain resilient and adaptable.

Examples in Continuity

To illustrate how these frameworks can complement the SMART method and each other, let's revisit some examples from earlier chapters.

Health:

- **SMART Goal:** "I want to lose 10 pounds in three months

by going to the gym three times a week and following a healthy diet."

- **OKR:** Objective: Improve overall fitness. Key Results: Track diet and exercise daily, achieve a 5% increase in muscle mass, reduce body fat percentage by 5% in three months.

- **BHAG:** "Complete an Ironman Triathlon within the next five years."

- **WOOP:** Wish: "I wish to lose weight and improve my health." Outcome: "I will feel more energetic and confident." Obstacle: "I might feel tempted to skip workouts or eat unhealthy foods." Plan: "If I feel tempted, then I will remind myself of my progress and choose a healthy alternative."

Career:

- **SMART Goal:** "I want to get a promotion to a managerial position within the next year by completing leadership training and taking on three new projects."

- **OKR:** Objective: Advance to a managerial role. Key Results: Complete leadership training program, mentor two junior employees, lead three major projects successfully.

- **BHAG:** "Become the CEO of my company within the

next 15 years."

- **WOOP:** Wish: "I wish to get a promotion to a managerial position." Outcome: "I will have greater responsibility and influence." Obstacle: "Balancing additional responsibilities with current workload." Plan: "If I feel overwhelmed, then I will delegate tasks and prioritize effectively."

Personal Growth:

- **SMART Goal:** "I want to read one book per month for the next year to enhance my knowledge."

- **OKR:** Objective: Enhance personal knowledge. Key Results: Read 12 books in a year, join a book club for discussions, write summaries for each book read.

- **BHAG:** "Write a book on my personal growth journey within the next decade."

- **WOOP:** Wish: "I wish to read more books." Outcome: "I will become more knowledgeable and well-rounded." Obstacle: "Finding time to read amidst a busy schedule." Plan: "If I struggle to find time, then I will allocate 30 minutes each night before bed for reading."

In this chapter, we've explored the OKR, BHAG, and WOOP frameworks, providing detailed explanations, benefits, and practical examples. These frameworks offer diverse strategies for setting and achieving goals, complementing the SMART method by addressing different aspects of goal setting and personal development.

As we continue our journey, we'll delve deeper into additional strategies and tools to further enhance your goal-setting process. By integrating these methods, you'll be equipped with a comprehensive toolkit to set, pursue, and achieve your most ambitious goals. Let's move forward with confidence, ready to transform our aspirations into reality.

6

VISION BOARDS AND VISUALIZATION

In the previous chapters, we explored various goal-setting frameworks, including the SMART method, OKRs, BHAGs, and WOOP. Now, let's dive into the power of visualization and vision boards. These tools can be incredibly effective in helping you manifest your goals by keeping them front and center in your mind. Visualization and vision boards tap into the psychological aspects of goal setting, enhancing your motivation and commitment.

Power of Visualization

Psychological Benefits

Visualization is a powerful mental technique that involves creating vivid images of your goals as if they have already been achieved. This process can significantly enhance your motivation and performance by engaging your brain in a way that aligns with your desired outcomes.

Dr. Richard Wiseman, a psychologist at the University of Hertfordshire, conducted a study that found people who visualize their goals are more likely to achieve them. Visualization activates the same neural pathways in the brain as actually performing the task, which can improve performance and reduce anxiety.

When you visualize your goals, you engage the creative subconscious, which starts generating ideas to achieve those goals. This mental rehearsal primes your brain for success, making you more likely to recognize and seize opportunities when they arise.

Visualization Techniques

1. **Mental Rehearsal:**

   ○ Imagine yourself successfully completing each step of your goal. For example, if your goal is to run a marathon, visualize yourself running each mile, feeling strong and confident. Picture the start line, the course, and the finish line in vivid detail.

2. **Positive Affirmations:**

   ○ Use positive statements to reinforce your belief in your

ability to achieve your goals. For instance, "I am capable of completing this project successfully." Repeating affirmations daily can help embed these positive beliefs into your subconscious mind.

3. Sensory Involvement:

○ Engage all your senses in the visualization process. Imagine the sights, sounds, smells, and feelings associated with achieving your goal. This makes the visualization more vivid and realistic. For example, if your goal is to give a successful presentation, visualize the room, hear your voice speaking confidently, and feel the clicker in your hand as you change slides.

4. Daily Practice:

○ Set aside a few minutes each day to visualize your goals. Consistent practice strengthens the neural pathways associated with your desired outcomes. Integrating visualization into your morning or evening routine can help reinforce your commitment to your goals.

A study by Dr. Blaslotto at the University of Chicago found that participants who visualized themselves making free throws improved their performance almost as much as those who actually practiced. This demonstrates the profound impact visualization can have on real-life performance.

Science Behind Visualization

Neuroscientific research supports the efficacy of visualization. When you visualize, your brain generates electrical impulses that replicate the ones created during the actual experience. This mental rehearsal activates your motor cortex, which enhances your ability to perform the visualized activities.

Dr. Stephen Kosslyn, a neuroscientist, found that visualization strengthens neural pathways, making it easier for you to perform the visualized tasks in reality. This process, known as neuroplasticity, allows your brain to adapt and improve based on your mental practice.

Creating Vision Boards

Vision boards are a tangible representation of your goals and aspirations. They serve as a constant visual reminder of what you're working towards, helping to keep you motivated and focused.

Materials and Tools Needed

Creating a vision board is a creative and personal process. Here are some materials and tools you might need:

- A large piece of poster board or corkboard

- Scissors, glue, and tape

- Magazines, printed images, or photos

- Markers, pens, and stickers

- Inspirational quotes or affirmations

- Optional: Digital tools (for creating a digital vision board)

Step-by-Step Guide to Creating a Vision Board

1. **Set Clear Goals:**

   ○ Before you start, take some time to think about your goals. What do you want to achieve in the next year? What are your long-term aspirations? Write down these goals to guide your vision board creation.

2. **Gather Materials:**

   ○ Collect magazines, images, quotes, and any other materials that resonate with your goals. Look for visuals that inspire and motivate you. Consider using a combination of images that represent your professional, personal, and health goals.

3. **Create a Positive Space:**

   ○ Find a quiet, comfortable space to work on your vision board. This should be a place where you feel relaxed and focused. Light a candle or play soft music to create a calming atmosphere.

4. Layout Your Board:

- Start by arranging your images and quotes on the board. There's no right or wrong way to do this – it's about what feels right for you. You can categorize your board by different areas of your life, such as career, health, and personal growth. Experiment with different layouts until you find one that feels balanced and inspiring.

5. Attach Your Images:

- Once you're happy with the layout, start gluing or taping the images and quotes to the board. Be creative and make it visually appealing. Use colorful markers and stickers to add personal touches and make your board unique.

6. Add Personal Touches:

- Use markers, stickers, or other decorations to personalize your board. You can write affirmations or key goals directly on the board. Adding your own handwriting and artistic elements can make the vision board feel more personal and powerful.

7. Place Your Vision Board in a Visible Location:

- Put your vision board somewhere you will see it every

day. This constant visual reminder will help keep your goals top of mind. Consider placing it near your workspace, in your bedroom, or anywhere you spend a lot of time.

8. **Regularly Update Your Board:**

   ○ As you achieve your goals or your aspirations evolve, feel free to update your vision board. This keeps it relevant and aligned with your current goals. Regularly refreshing your vision board can reinvigorate your motivation and commitment.

Success Stories

Visualization and vision boards have helped many individuals achieve remarkable goals. Here are some inspiring success stories that demonstrate the power of these tools.

Success Story: Oprah Winfrey

Oprah Winfrey, one of the most successful media moguls in the world, has often spoken about the power of visualization. She used visualization to envision her success long before it became a reality. Oprah credits much of her success to her ability to see her goals clearly in her mind and believe in her ability to achieve them.

Oprah's journey from a challenging childhood to becoming a global icon is a testament to the power of visualization. She often visualized herself as a successful talk show host, influencing and inspiring millions. This mental rehearsal helped her stay focused and motivated, even in the face of obstacles.

Success Story: Jim Carrey

Jim Carrey, the famous actor and comedian, is another advocate of visualization. In the early 1990s, before he was a household name, Carrey wrote himself a check for $10 million for "acting services rendered" and dated it for Thanksgiving 1995. He kept the check in his wallet and visualized himself receiving that amount for a movie role. In 1994, he received a $10 million contract for his role in "Dumb and Dumber," just as he had envisioned.

Carrey's story highlights the importance of specificity in visualization. By setting a clear and specific financial goal, he was able to direct his energy and efforts towards achieving it. His success demonstrates how visualization can turn ambitious dreams into reality.

Success Story: Sarah Centrella

Sarah Centrella, a bestselling author and motivational speaker, transformed her life using vision boards. After experiencing a personal crisis, she created vision boards to visualize her goals and dreams. Sarah attributes her success to the clarity and motivation provided by her vision boards, which helped her achieve goals such as becoming a published author, traveling the world, and building a successful coaching business.

Centrella's use of vision boards allowed her to maintain focus and motivation during challenging times. By visually representing her goals, she kept her aspirations at the forefront of her mind, driving her to take consistent action towards achieving them.

Success Story: John Assaraf

John Assaraf, a successful entrepreneur and author, has a well-known story about the power of vision boards. In the early 1990s, Assaraf created a vision board that included a picture of his dream home. Five years later, while unpacking after moving into a new house, he discovered that the home he had just purchased was the exact one he had placed on his vision board years earlier. This powerful example demonstrates how visualization can help manifest specific and tangible outcomes.

Assaraf's experience underscores the importance of visual clarity in goal setting. By clearly envisioning his dream home, he was able to align his actions and decisions with that vision, ultimately turning it into reality.

Success Story: Lindsey Vonn

Olympic skier Lindsey Vonn used visualization to prepare for her races. She would visualize herself skiing the course, mentally rehearsing each turn and jump. This practice helped her build confidence and improve her performance. Vonn's dedication to visualization contributed to her becoming one of the most successful female skiers in history.

Vonn's story illustrates how visualization can enhance performance in high-pressure situations. By mentally rehearsing her races, she prepared her mind and body for success, enabling her to perform at her best when it mattered most.

Practical Applications and Studies

Practical Tips for Effective Visualization

1. **Consistency:**

   - Make visualization a daily habit. Consistency is key to reinforcing the neural pathways associated with your goals.

2. **Clarity:**

   - Be specific about what you want to achieve. The clearer your visualization, the more effective it will be.

3. **Emotion:**

   - Engage your emotions during visualization. Feel the excitement, pride, and joy of achieving your goal. Emotional engagement makes the visualization more powerful.

4. Detail:

- ○ Include as many details as possible. The more vivid and detailed your visualization, the more your brain will perceive it as real.

Scientific Studies Supporting Visualization

1. Study by Dr. Blaslotto:

- ○ As mentioned earlier, Dr. Blaslotto's study at the University of Chicago found that basketball players who visualized making free throws improved their performance almost as much as those who actually practiced. This study highlights the effectiveness of mental rehearsal.

2. Study by Dr. Richard Wiseman:

- ○ Dr. Wiseman's research on visualization found that people who visualize their goals are more likely to achieve them. Visualization engages the brain's neural pathways, making the imagined experience almost as real as the actual one.

3. Study by Dr. Stephen Kosslyn:

- ○ Dr. Kosslyn's research on neuroplasticity demonstrates that visualization can strengthen neural pathways, enhancing your ability to perform the visualized activities. This process of mental rehearsal prepares your brain for success.

4. **Study by Dr. Gabriele Oettingen:**

○ Dr. Oettingen's research on mental contrasting and the WOOP method found that combining visualization with realistic planning significantly increases the likelihood of achieving goals. By anticipating obstacles and planning for them, individuals can maintain motivation and resilience.

Conclusion

In this chapter, we've explored the power of visualization and vision boards, understanding how these tools can significantly enhance your ability to achieve your goals. Visualization engages your brain's neural pathways, making the imagined experience almost as real as the actual one. This mental rehearsal can improve performance, boost motivation, and increase confidence.

Creating a vision board provides a tangible and constant reminder of your goals, helping to keep you focused and inspired. By surrounding yourself with images and quotes that represent your aspirations, you reinforce your commitment to achieving them.

As you continue your journey of goal setting and achievement, consider incorporating visualization and vision boards into your routine. These tools can complement the SMART method, OKRs, BHAGs, and WOOP, providing a comprehensive approach to realizing your dreams.

Remember, the power to achieve your goals lies within you. By visualizing your success and keeping your aspirations in sight, you can turn your dreams into reality. Let's move forward with confidence, using every tool at our disposal to create the life we envision.

7

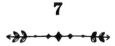

WRITING DOWN YOUR GOALS

In the previous chapters, we explored various methods and tools for setting and achieving goals, including the power of visualization and vision boards. Now, let's delve into the importance of writing down your goals. Documenting your goals is a critical step in the goal-setting process that can significantly enhance your ability to achieve them. In this chapter, we'll examine the psychological benefits of writing goals, explore journaling techniques, and discuss digital tools that can aid in goal tracking.

Importance of Documentation

Psychological Benefits of Writing Goals

Writing down your goals transforms your intentions into tangible commitments. This simple act has profound psychological benefits that can boost your motivation, focus, and likelihood of success.

1. **Clarity and Focus:**

   ○ Writing goals down clarifies your intentions, making them more concrete and specific. This clarity helps you focus on what you truly want to achieve. Research by Dr. Gail Matthews at the Dominican University of California found that people who write down their goals are 42% more likely to achieve them compared to those who only think about their goals.

2. **Commitment and Accountability:**

   ○ Putting your goals in writing creates a sense of commitment and accountability. It's a declaration of your intention to pursue these goals, making it harder to dismiss or forget them. This commitment is reinforced when you regularly review your written goals.

3. **Visual Reminder:**

   ○ Written goals serve as a constant visual reminder of what you're working towards. This reminder keeps your goals at the forefront of your mind, helping you stay motivated and focused.

4. Emotional Connection:

- The act of writing engages different parts of your brain, deepening your emotional connection to your goals. This connection enhances your intrinsic motivation, making you more likely to persevere in the face of challenges.

5. Cognitive Processing:

- Writing down your goals involves cognitive processing that can help solidify your intentions and plans. This processing aids in the development of actionable steps and strategies for achieving your goals.

Dr. Matthews' study also found that individuals who wrote down their goals and shared them with a friend achieved even greater success. This finding highlights the importance of both documentation and social support in the goal-setting process.

Journaling Techniques

Daily, Weekly, and Monthly Goal Journaling

Journaling is a versatile and powerful tool for documenting and tracking your goals. Regular journaling helps you monitor your progress, reflect on your experiences, and stay accountable. Here are some effective journaling techniques:

1. **Daily Journaling:**

- **Morning Entries:**

  - Start your day by writing down your goals and intentions. This practice sets a positive and focused tone for the day. Include specific actions you plan to take to move closer to your goals.

  - Example: "Today, I will spend one hour on my marketing project to increase my business visibility."

- **Evening Reflections:**

  - End your day with reflections on your progress. Note any achievements, challenges, and insights. This practice helps you stay accountable and recognize your daily efforts.

  - Example: "I completed my marketing tasks today and made significant progress. I faced some challenges with time management, which I'll work on improving tomorrow."

2. **Weekly Journaling:**

○ **Weekly Reviews:**

- Set aside time at the end of each week to review your progress and plan for the upcoming week. Reflect on what worked, what didn't, and any adjustments needed.

- Example: "This week, I met my fitness goals by working out three times. I struggled with maintaining my diet, so I'll plan my meals better next week."

○ **Goal Setting:**

- Use your weekly journal to set specific goals for the upcoming week. Break down larger goals into smaller, actionable steps.

- Example: "Next week, I will complete the first draft of my book chapter and review it with my writing group."

3. **Monthly Journaling:**

○ **Monthly Overviews:**

- At the end of each month, review your overall progress. Assess how well you met your goals and identify any patterns or areas for improvement.

- Example: "This month, I achieved my fitness goals and made good progress on my book. I need to focus more on my professional development goals next month."

  ◦ **Goal Adjustments:**

  - Adjust your goals based on your monthly reflections. Set new goals for the upcoming month that align with your long-term aspirations.

  - Example: "Next month, I will attend a professional workshop and increase my networking efforts to advance my career."

Reflective Journaling Practices

Reflective journaling involves deeper introspection and analysis of your experiences and progress. This practice helps you gain insights and learn from your journey.

1. **Gratitude Journaling:**

   ◦ Regularly write about things you're grateful for, especially related to your goals. This practice fosters a positive mindset and helps you stay motivated.

   ◦ Example: "I'm grateful for the support of my family in pursuing my fitness goals. Their encouragement keeps me going."

2. **Overcoming Challenges:**

- Reflect on the obstacles you've faced and how you overcame them. This practice builds resilience and problem-solving skills.

- Example: "I struggled with time management this week but overcame it by setting stricter schedules. This taught me the importance of planning."

3. **Success Stories:**

- Document your successes and milestones. Celebrate your achievements and reflect on the strategies that led to your success.

- Example: "I completed my first marathon today! Consistent training and support from my running group were key to my success."

Digital Tools

Apps and Software for Goal Tracking

In addition to traditional journaling, digital tools offer a convenient and efficient way to document and track your goals. Here are some popular apps and software for goal tracking:

1. Trello:

- Trello is a versatile project management tool that allows you to create boards, lists, and cards to organize your goals and tasks. You can set deadlines, add checklists, and collaborate with others.

- Example: Use Trello to create a board for your fitness goals, with lists for daily workouts, meal plans, and progress tracking.

2. Evernote:

- Evernote is a note-taking app that helps you capture ideas, create to-do lists, and organize your thoughts. You can use it to write down your goals, track your progress, and store related resources.

- Example: Use Evernote to document your professional development goals, including notes from workshops and articles you want to read.

3. Habitica:

- Habitica turns goal tracking into a game. You create a character and earn rewards for completing tasks and goals. This app adds an element of fun and accountability to your goal-setting process.

- Example: Use Habitica to track daily habits such as

exercising, reading, and meditating. Earn points and rewards as you achieve your goals.

4. **Notion:**

- Notion is an all-in-one workspace that allows you to create databases, notes, calendars, and more. It's highly customizable and can be tailored to your specific goal-tracking needs.

- Example: Use Notion to create a dashboard for your writing goals, with sections for brainstorming, outlining, and tracking your word count progress.

5. **Google Keep:**

- Google Keep is a simple note-taking app that allows you to create and share notes, lists, and reminders. It's integrated with other Google services, making it easy to access across devices.

- Example: Use Google Keep to set daily reminders for your personal growth goals, such as practicing a new skill or reading a book.

Advantages of Digital Goal-Setting Tools

1. **Accessibility:**

- Digital tools are accessible from multiple devices, allowing you to update and review your goals anytime, anywhere. This convenience ensures that your goals are always within reach.

2. **Organization:**

- Digital tools offer various organizational features, such as tags, categories, and reminders. These features help you keep your goals and tasks organized and easily manageable.

3. **Collaboration:**

- Many digital tools allow for collaboration, enabling you to share your goals with friends, family, or colleagues. This feature fosters accountability and support from others.

4. **Integration:**

- Digital tools often integrate with other apps and services, streamlining your workflow and making it easier to manage your goals alongside other responsibilities.

5. **Tracking and Analytics:**

- Digital tools provide tracking and analytics features that allow you to monitor your progress and identify trends. These insights can help you make informed adjustments to your goals and strategies.

A study by Dr. Mike Morrison from the University of Groningen found that using digital tools for goal tracking can enhance motivation and productivity. The study highlighted the benefits of features such as reminders, progress tracking, and collaborative elements in maintaining goal commitment.

Practical Applications and Studies

Practical Tips for Effective Goal Documentation

1. **Set Clear and Specific Goals:**

   ○ Ensure your goals are specific, measurable, achievable, relevant, and time-bound (SMART). Clear goals are easier to document and track.

2. **Regularly Review and Update Goals:**

   ○ Make it a habit to review and update your goals regularly. This practice keeps your goals relevant and aligned with your evolving aspirations.

3. **Use a Combination of Tools:**

   ○ Combine traditional journaling with digital tools to leverage the benefits of both. Use a journal for reflective practices and digital tools for organization and tracking.

4. Share Your Goals:

○ Share your goals with a trusted friend, mentor, or accountability partner. This social support can enhance your commitment and provide valuable feedback.

Scientific Studies Supporting Goal Documentation

1. Study by Dr. Gail Matthews:

○ Dr. Matthews' research found that individuals who write down their goals and share them with a friend are more likely to achieve them. This study highlights the importance of documentation and social support in the goal-setting process.

2. Study by Dr. Robert S. Rubin:

○ Dr. Rubin's research emphasizes the benefits of measurable goals. Writing down specific criteria for success helps individuals track their progress and stay motivated.

3. Study by Dr. Mike Morrison:

○ Dr. Morrison's study on digital tools for goal tracking found that features such as reminders, progress tracking, and collaboration enhance motivation and productivity. Digital tools offer convenience and organization that support goal achievement.

4. **Study by Dr. Stephen Kosslyn:**

- Dr. Kosslyn's research on cognitive processing shows that writing down goals engages the brain in ways that solidify intentions and plans. This cognitive engagement enhances goal clarity and commitment.

Conclusion

In this chapter, we've explored the importance of writing down your goals, examining the psychological benefits, journaling techniques, and digital tools that can aid in goal tracking. Documenting your goals transforms your intentions into tangible commitments, enhancing clarity, focus, and motivation.

Journaling provides a versatile and reflective approach to goal documentation, allowing you to monitor your progress, reflect on your experiences, and stay accountable. Digital tools offer convenience, organization, and collaboration features that complement traditional journaling practices.

By incorporating these practices and tools into your goal-setting routine, you can significantly enhance your ability to achieve your goals. The act of writing down your goals, whether in a journal or digital app, reinforces your commitment and provides a constant reminder of what you're working towards.

As you continue your journey of goal setting and achievement, remember that the power to achieve your goals lies within you. By documenting your goals and regularly reviewing them, you can turn your aspirations into reality. Let's move forward with confidence, using every tool at our disposal to create the life we envision.

PART 3

Achieving Your Goals

8

CREATING ACTION PLANS

In the previous chapters, we explored various goal-setting frameworks, visualization techniques, and the importance of writing down your goals. Now, let's delve into the practical aspects of achieving your goals. Creating an action plan is a crucial step in turning your aspirations into reality. This chapter will cover the importance of breaking down goals into actionable steps, techniques for prioritizing tasks, and methods for setting realistic deadlines.

Breaking Down Goals

Importance of Actionable Steps

Setting a goal is only the beginning. To achieve it, you need a clear plan of action. Breaking down your goals into smaller, actionable steps makes them more manageable and less overwhelming. This approach helps you maintain focus, track progress, and stay motivated.

Research by Dr. Gail Matthews at the Dominican University of California found that people who not only wrote down their goals but also created action plans were significantly more likely to achieve them. This study highlights the importance of detailed planning in the goal-setting process.

Methods for Breaking Down Large Goals

1. **Mind Mapping:**

   ○ Mind mapping is a visual tool that helps you break down a large goal into smaller, interconnected tasks. Start with your main goal in the center and branch out into smaller tasks and sub-tasks. This method provides a clear overview of everything that needs to be done.

   ○ Example: If your goal is to write a book, your mind map might include branches for research, outlining, writing, editing, and publishing.

2. **Task Lists:**

   ○ Create a detailed task list that outlines each step required to achieve your goal. Breaking your goal into smaller tasks makes it easier to focus on one thing at a time and track your progress.

○ Example: For a fitness goal, your task list might include joining a gym, creating a workout schedule, buying appropriate gear, and tracking your workouts.

3. Gantt Charts:

○ Gantt charts are a project management tool that helps you visualize your tasks over time. They provide a timeline for each task, showing start and end dates, dependencies, and milestones.

○ Example: For a professional project, a Gantt chart can help you map out each phase, from initial planning to final execution, ensuring you stay on schedule.

4. Backwards Planning:

○ Start with your end goal and work backwards to identify the steps needed to achieve it. This method ensures that you consider all necessary actions and can be particularly useful for complex goals.

○ Example: If your goal is to run a marathon, you might start by identifying the race date, then work backwards to plan your training schedule, including key milestones like running a half-marathon.

5. **SMART Breakdown:**

- Apply the SMART criteria to break down your goal into specific, measurable, achievable, relevant, and time-bound steps. This method ensures each task is clear and actionable.

- Example: For a career advancement goal, your SMART breakdown might include specific tasks like completing a certification, networking with industry professionals, and applying for new positions.

Prioritizing Tasks

Techniques for Prioritization

Once you have broken down your goals into actionable steps, the next challenge is to prioritize these tasks. Effective prioritization ensures that you focus on the most important tasks first, making efficient use of your time and resources.

Eisenhower Matrix:

The Eisenhower Matrix, also known as the Urgent-Important Matrix, is a powerful tool for prioritizing tasks based on their urgency and importance. It divides tasks into four categories:

1. **Urgent and Important (Do First):**

○ These tasks require immediate attention and are critical to achieving your goals. Prioritize these tasks to prevent crises and ensure steady progress.

○ Example: If you're working on a deadline for a work project, tasks like completing key reports or presentations fall into this category.

2. Important but Not Urgent (Schedule):

○ These tasks are essential for long-term success but don't require immediate action. Schedule time to work on these tasks to prevent them from becoming urgent.

○ Example: Long-term projects like writing a book or developing a new skill should be scheduled regularly to ensure progress.

3. Urgent but Not Important (Delegate):

○ These tasks demand immediate attention but don't significantly contribute to your long-term goals. Delegate these tasks if possible.

○ Example: Routine administrative tasks or minor interruptions that can be handled by someone else fall into this category.

4. Not Urgent and Not Important (Eliminate):

- These tasks are distractions that don't contribute to your goals. Minimize or eliminate these tasks to free up time for more important activities.

- Example: Excessive social media use or other time-wasting activities should be limited or avoided.

ABC Method:

The ABC method involves categorizing tasks based on their priority level:

1. **A Tasks:**

    - High-priority tasks that are critical to achieving your goals. Focus on these tasks first.

    - Example: Completing a major work project or preparing for an important presentation.

2. **B Tasks:**

    - Medium-priority tasks that are important but not as urgent as A tasks. Schedule time to address these tasks after completing A tasks.

    - Example: Ongoing training or professional development activities.

3. **C Tasks:**

- Low-priority tasks that are neither urgent nor important. These tasks can be addressed after A and B tasks or eliminated if they are not necessary.

- Example: Organizing files or other routine maintenance tasks.

Pareto Principle (80/20 Rule):

The Pareto Principle states that 80% of your results come from 20% of your efforts. Identify the key tasks that have the greatest impact on your goals and focus on those tasks.

1. **Identify High-Impact Tasks:**

   - Determine which tasks contribute the most to your goals and prioritize them.

   - Example: If your goal is to increase sales, focus on high-impact activities like reaching out to key clients or improving your sales pitch.

2. **Minimize Low-Impact Tasks:**

   - Reduce the time spent on tasks that have minimal impact on your goals.

   - Example: Limit administrative work or other tasks that do not directly contribute to your main objectives.

Setting Deadlines

Importance of Timelines

Setting deadlines is crucial for maintaining momentum and ensuring steady progress towards your goals. Deadlines create a sense of urgency and help you stay focused and organized.

Research by Dr. Dan Ariely, a behavioral economist at Duke University, found that self-imposed deadlines can be highly effective in improving performance and reducing procrastination. However, these deadlines must be realistic and well-structured to be effective.

How to Set Realistic Deadlines

1. **Assess the Scope of the Task:**

   - Understand the full scope of the task and estimate the time required to complete it. Consider potential challenges and allocate extra time for unforeseen obstacles.

   - Example: If your goal is to launch a new product, assess the time needed for research, development, testing, and marketing.

2. **Break Down the Task:**

   - Divide the task into smaller, manageable steps, each

with its own deadline. This approach ensures steady progress and prevents feeling overwhelmed.

○ Example: For a fitness goal, set deadlines for smaller milestones like losing a certain amount of weight each month or completing specific workouts each week.

3. Set Specific Deadlines:

○ Assign specific dates to each task and sub-task. Clear deadlines help you stay on track and measure your progress.

○ Example: "Complete the first draft of my book by June 30th" is more effective than "Finish my book soon."

4. Prioritize Deadlines:

○ Prioritize deadlines based on the importance and urgency of the tasks. Use the Eisenhower Matrix or ABC method to help prioritize.

○ Example: Prioritize urgent project tasks with earlier deadlines over long-term goals with flexible timelines.

5. Monitor and Adjust:

○ Regularly review your progress and adjust deadlines as needed. Be flexible and willing to adapt your plan based on new information or changing circumstances.

○ Example: If you encounter unexpected challenges, adjust your deadlines to ensure you stay on track without compromising the quality of your work.

Practical Applications and Studies

Implementing Action Plans in Real-Life

1. Health and Fitness Goals:

○ **Breaking Down Goals:**

- Goal: Run a marathon in one year.

- Action Plan: Create a training schedule, join a running club, track progress weekly, and adjust training as needed.

○ **Prioritizing Tasks:**

- Use the ABC method to prioritize training sessions, rest days, and nutrition planning.

○ **Setting Deadlines:**

- Set monthly milestones for distance and pace improvements. Example: "Run a half-marathon in six months as a milestone."

2. Career Advancement Goals:

○ Breaking Down Goals:

- Goal: Get promoted to a managerial position within two years.

- Action Plan: Complete leadership training, take on additional responsibilities, network with senior management, and seek feedback regularly.

○ Prioritizing Tasks:

- Use the Eisenhower Matrix to prioritize urgent tasks like current job responsibilities and important tasks like professional development.

○ Setting Deadlines:

- Set quarterly deadlines for completing training modules and annual deadlines for performance reviews. Example: "Complete leadership certification by the end of the first year."

3. Personal Development Goals:

○ Breaking Down Goals:

- Goal: Learn a new language in one year.

- Action Plan: Enroll in a language course, practice

daily with language apps, join a language exchange group, and set specific learning milestones.

○ **Prioritizing Tasks:**

  • Apply the Pareto Principle to focus on high-impact activities like speaking practice and immersive experiences.

○ **Setting Deadlines:**

  • Set weekly and monthly milestones for vocabulary acquisition and conversational practice. Example: "Learn 100 new words each month."

Scientific Studies Supporting Action Plans

1. **Study by Dr. Gail Matthews:**

  ○ Dr. Matthews' research found that creating detailed action plans significantly increases the likelihood of achieving goals. This study emphasizes the importance of breaking down goals into actionable steps.

2. **Study by Dr. Dan Ariely:**

  ○ Dr. Ariely's research on self-imposed deadlines highlights the effectiveness of setting specific, realistic deadlines in improving performance and reducing procrastination. Clear deadlines create a sense of urgency and accountability.

3. **Study by Dr. Edwin Locke:**

○ Dr. Locke's goal-setting theory emphasizes the importance of setting specific, challenging goals. Breaking down these goals into smaller tasks and setting deadlines enhances motivation and performance.

Conclusion

In this chapter, we've explored the crucial steps of creating action plans, prioritizing tasks, and setting realistic deadlines. Breaking down your goals into actionable steps makes them more manageable and less overwhelming, ensuring steady progress and sustained motivation.

Effective prioritization techniques, such as the Eisenhower Matrix, ABC method, and Pareto Principle, help you focus on the most important tasks first. Setting realistic deadlines creates a sense of urgency and helps you stay organized and on track.

By implementing these strategies, you can turn your goals into actionable plans and achieve them systematically. Remember, the journey to achieving your goals begins with a single step. Let's take that step together, using the power of action plans, prioritization, and deadlines to turn your aspirations into reality.

As we continue our journey, we'll explore additional strategies and tools to further enhance your goal achievement process. Stay focused, stay committed, and let's achieve greatness together.

9

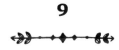

OVERCOMING OBSTACLES

In the previous chapter, we discussed the importance of creating action plans, prioritizing tasks, and setting realistic deadlines. However, even with the best-laid plans, obstacles are inevitable. In this chapter, we'll explore common obstacles in goal achievement, techniques to maintain motivation, and inspirational stories of resilience and overcoming adversity. Understanding these elements will equip you with the tools and mindset necessary to navigate challenges and achieve your goals.

Identifying Challenges

Common Obstacles in Goal Achievement

1. **Procrastination:**

○ One of the most common obstacles is procrastination. Delaying tasks can derail your progress and make goals seem unattainable. Research by Dr. Piers Steel, a professor of motivational psychology, found that procrastination affects up to 20% of people chronically, impacting their ability to achieve goals.

2. Lack of Resources:

○ Sometimes, achieving a goal requires resources such as time, money, or expertise that you may not have readily available. This scarcity can hinder your progress and create frustration.

3. Fear of Failure:

○ The fear of failing can be paralyzing, preventing you from taking necessary steps towards your goal. Dr. Carol Dweck's research on mindset highlights that individuals with a fixed mindset are more likely to fear failure and avoid challenges, whereas those with a growth mindset embrace challenges as opportunities to learn.

4. Distractions:

○ In today's digital age, distractions are everywhere. Whether it's social media, emails, or other interruptions, staying focused on your goals can be challenging.

5. Lack of Motivation:

- Maintaining consistent motivation can be difficult, especially when progress is slow or obstacles seem insurmountable. Motivation can wane over time, making it harder to stay committed to your goals.

6. Negative Self-Talk:

- Self-doubt and negative self-talk can undermine your confidence and prevent you from taking action. Cognitive-behavioral research shows that negative thoughts can significantly impact your ability to achieve goals.

7. Physical and Mental Health Issues:

- Health problems can pose significant challenges to achieving goals. Physical ailments can limit your ability to perform tasks, while mental health issues like anxiety and depression can reduce your motivation and focus.

8. External Circumstances:

- External factors such as economic downturns, natural disasters, or personal emergencies can create unforeseen obstacles that disrupt your plans.

Example Continuation:

Let's revisit the example of training for a marathon. You might face obstacles like injuries (physical health issues), a busy schedule (lack of time), or doubts about your ability to complete the race (negative self-talk). Identifying these challenges early on can help you develop strategies to overcome them.

Staying Motivated

Techniques to Maintain Motivation

1. **Setting Incremental Goals:**

   - Break down your larger goal into smaller, incremental goals. This approach provides a sense of accomplishment as you achieve each milestone, keeping you motivated.

   - Example: Instead of focusing solely on running a full marathon, set smaller goals like running a 5K, then a 10K, and so on.

2. **Reward Systems:**

   - Implement a reward system to celebrate your achievements. Rewards can provide positive reinforcement and make the process enjoyable.

○ Example: Treat yourself to a new pair of running shoes after reaching a certain milestone in your training.

3. Accountability Partners:

○ Find an accountability partner who can support and motivate you. Sharing your progress and challenges with someone else can keep you on track.

○ Example: Partner with a friend who also wants to improve their fitness, and check in with each other regularly.

4. Visualization:

○ Use visualization techniques to keep your goal vivid in your mind. Regularly visualize the successful achievement of your goal to boost your motivation.

○ Example: Visualize crossing the marathon finish line, feeling strong and accomplished.

5. Positive Affirmations:

○ Use positive affirmations to reinforce your belief in your ability to achieve your goals. Replace negative self-talk with empowering statements.

○ Example: "I am capable of running this marathon and achieving my fitness goals."

6. Mindfulness and Meditation:

- Practice mindfulness and meditation to reduce stress and improve focus. These practices can help you stay present and motivated.

- Example: Incorporate a daily meditation routine to clear your mind and refocus on your training goals.

7. Adjusting Goals:

- Be flexible and willing to adjust your goals as needed. If you encounter significant obstacles, modifying your goals can help maintain motivation.

- Example: If you suffer an injury, adjust your training plan to include low-impact exercises until you recover.

8. Tracking Progress:

- Regularly track your progress to see how far you've come. Keeping a record of your achievements can boost your motivation and help you stay focused.

- Example: Maintain a training journal where you log your runs, distances, and how you feel after each session.

Example Continuation:

In the marathon training example, you can stay motivated by setting incremental goals like completing shorter races, rewarding yourself with new gear, finding a training partner, and visualizing your success. These techniques help maintain motivation and ensure you stay committed to your training plan.

Resilience Stories

Inspirational Stories of Overcoming Adversity

Story 1: J.K. Rowling

J.K. Rowling, the author of the Harry Potter series, faced numerous obstacles before achieving success. She wrote the first book as a single mother living on welfare. Rowling's manuscript was rejected by 12 publishers before Bloomsbury accepted it. Despite financial struggles and repeated rejections, she persisted and ultimately became one of the best-selling authors in history. Her story illustrates the power of resilience and determination.

Story 2: Thomas Edison

Thomas Edison, one of the greatest inventors of all time, faced countless failures on his path to success. Edison famously failed thousands of times before successfully inventing the electric light bulb. His resilience and refusal to give up exemplify the importance of perseverance in overcoming obstacles.

Story 3: Oprah Winfrey

Oprah Winfrey overcame significant adversity to become a media mogul and philanthropist. Born into poverty and experiencing numerous personal hardships, including abuse and discrimination, Winfrey used her challenges as motivation. She worked tirelessly to build her career, eventually becoming one of the most influential women in the world. Her story highlights how resilience can turn obstacles into stepping stones for success.

Story 4: Nick Vujicic

Nick Vujicic was born without arms and legs due to a rare condition called tetra-amelia syndrome. Despite his physical limitations, Vujicic became a motivational speaker, author, and founder of the non-profit organization Life Without Limbs. He travels the world inspiring millions with his message of hope and overcoming adversity. Vujicic's story demonstrates that no obstacle is insurmountable with the right mindset and determination.

Story 5: Malala Yousafzai

Malala Yousafzai, a Pakistani activist for female education, faced life-threatening adversity when she was shot by the Taliban for advocating for girls' education. Despite the attack, Malala continued her activism and became the youngest-ever Nobel Prize laureate. Her resilience and courage in the face of extreme danger have inspired people worldwide to stand up for their rights and pursue their goals despite significant risks.

Example Continuation:

Returning to our marathon training example, consider the story of Harriette Thompson, who began running marathons at the age of 76 and became the oldest woman to complete a marathon at 92. Despite battling cancer and facing numerous health challenges, she remained committed to her goal. Her story can serve as a powerful source of inspiration, reminding you that it's never too late to pursue your dreams and overcome obstacles.

Practical Applications and Studies

Implementing Resilience Techniques

1. **Developing a Growth Mindset:**

   - Embrace challenges as opportunities to learn and grow. Dr. Carol Dweck's research on growth mindset shows that viewing obstacles as learning experiences can increase resilience.

   - Example: If you encounter a setback in your marathon training, view it as a chance to improve your strategy and become a better runner.

2. **Building a Support Network:**

   - Surround yourself with supportive people who encourage and motivate you. A strong support network can provide the emotional strength needed to overcome obstacles.

- ○ Example: Join a running club or online community where members share their experiences and support each other's goals.

3. **Practicing Self-Compassion:**

- ○ Be kind to yourself when facing difficulties. Self-compassion can reduce stress and improve resilience, helping you stay motivated.

- ○ Example: If you miss a training session, avoid self-criticism and instead focus on getting back on track the next day.

4. **Setting Realistic Expectations:**

- ○ Set achievable goals and manage your expectations. Realistic goals prevent frustration and help maintain motivation.

- ○ Example: If running a full marathon feels too daunting, start with a half-marathon and gradually increase your distance.

5. **Creating a Contingency Plan:**

- Plan for potential obstacles and have backup strategies in place. A contingency plan can help you stay on course despite setbacks.

- Example: If bad weather prevents outdoor training, have an indoor workout routine ready to maintain your fitness.

Scientific Studies Supporting Resilience

1. **Study by Dr. Angela Duckworth:**

   - Dr. Duckworth's research on grit, which combines passion and perseverance, highlights the importance of resilience in achieving long-term goals. Her studies show that grit is a better predictor of success than talent.

2. **Study by Dr. Carol Dweck:**

   - Dr. Dweck's research on growth mindset demonstrates that individuals who believe their abilities can be developed through effort are more likely to overcome obstacles and achieve their goals.

3. **Study by Dr. Martin Seligman:**

   - Dr. Seligman's work on positive psychology and resilience shows that individuals who practice optimism and positive thinking are better equipped to handle adversity and achieve their goals.

Conclusion

In this chapter, we've explored the common obstacles that can hinder goal achievement, techniques to maintain motivation, and inspiring stories of resilience. Overcoming obstacles is an inevitable part of the journey towards achieving your goals. By identifying challenges early on, you can develop strategies to address them effectively.

Maintaining motivation through techniques like setting incremental goals, rewarding yourself, and finding accountability partners can keep you on track. Drawing inspiration from resilience stories reminds you that challenges can be overcome with determination and a positive mindset.

By implementing resilience techniques and leveraging the insights from scientific studies, you can build the mental strength needed to navigate obstacles and stay committed to your goals. Remember, every setback is an opportunity to learn and grow. Let's continue our journey with resilience and determination, ready to overcome any obstacle that comes our way.

As we move forward, we'll explore additional strategies and tools to further enhance your goal achievement process. Stay focused, stay resilient, and let's achieve greatness together.

10

TIME MANAGEMENT AND PRODUCTIVITY

In the previous chapters, we discussed overcoming obstacles and maintaining motivation on your journey toward achieving your goals. Now, let's focus on effective time management and productivity, essential skills for anyone striving to reach their objectives. In this chapter, we'll explore time management strategies, productivity hacks, and techniques for balancing multiple goals simultaneously.

Effective Time Management

Time Management Strategies

Effective time management is crucial for achieving your goals. It helps you allocate your time efficiently, prioritize tasks, and reduce stress. Here are some proven time management strategies:

1. **Pomodoro Technique:**

- The Pomodoro Technique, developed by Francesco Cirillo, involves breaking your work into 25-minute intervals, called "Pomodoros," with short breaks in between. After four Pomodoros, take a longer break. This method helps maintain focus and prevent burnout.

- **Example:** If you're writing a book, set a timer for 25 minutes and focus solely on writing. After the timer goes off, take a 5-minute break before starting the next Pomodoro.

2. **Eisenhower Matrix:**

- The Eisenhower Matrix helps you prioritize tasks based on their urgency and importance. It divides tasks into four categories: urgent and important, important but not urgent, urgent but not important, and neither urgent nor important. This strategy ensures you focus on what truly matters.

- **Example:** If you're juggling work and fitness goals, use the matrix to prioritize tasks like preparing for an important meeting (urgent and important) and scheduling workouts (important but not urgent).

3. Time Blocking:

- Time blocking involves scheduling specific blocks of time for different tasks or activities. This method helps you dedicate focused periods to your goals, minimizing distractions and interruptions.

- **Example:** Block off 9 AM to 11 AM each day for focused work on your side project, ensuring no other tasks interfere with this time.

4. Pareto Principle (80/20 Rule):

- The Pareto Principle states that 80% of your results come from 20% of your efforts. Identify the tasks that have the most significant impact on your goals and prioritize them.

- **Example:** If you're running a business, focus on high-impact tasks like strategic planning and client meetings rather than administrative work.

5. Getting Things Done (GTD):

- GTD, created by David Allen, involves capturing all tasks, organizing them, and regularly reviewing and prioritizing them. This method ensures nothing falls through the cracks and helps you stay organized.

- ○ **Example:** Use a GTD app to capture all your tasks and organize them by project, context, and priority.

Productivity Hacks

Tips for Increasing Productivity

Maximizing productivity is about working smarter, not harder. Here are some productivity hacks to help you achieve more in less time:

1. **Batching Tasks:**

   - ○ Group similar tasks together and complete them in one session. This reduces the cognitive load of switching between different types of tasks and improves efficiency.

   - ○ **Example:** Instead of responding to emails throughout the day, dedicate one or two specific times for email management.

2. **Eliminating Distractions:**

   - ○ Identify and eliminate distractions that hinder your productivity. This might involve turning off notifications, creating a dedicated workspace, or using apps that block distracting websites.

- **Example:** Use a website blocker to prevent access to social media during work hours, allowing you to focus on your tasks.

3. Using the Two-Minute Rule:

- If a task takes less than two minutes to complete, do it immediately. This prevents small tasks from piling up and becoming overwhelming.

- **Example:** Respond to a quick email or file a document as soon as it comes to your attention.

4. Practicing Mindfulness:

- Mindfulness techniques, such as meditation, can improve focus and reduce stress. Incorporating mindfulness into your routine can enhance overall productivity.

- **Example:** Start your day with a 10-minute mindfulness meditation to clear your mind and set a focused tone for the day.

5. Delegating Tasks:

- Delegate tasks that others can handle, freeing up your

time for high-priority activities. Effective delegation involves clear communication and trust in your team or collaborators.

- ○ **Example:** Delegate routine tasks like data entry or scheduling meetings to an assistant, allowing you to focus on strategic planning.

6. **Implementing the Ivy Lee Method:**

- ○ At the end of each day, write down the six most important tasks you need to accomplish the next day, in order of priority. Focus on completing each task in sequence.

- ○ **Example:** List your top six tasks for tomorrow, such as completing a client proposal, preparing a presentation, and making follow-up calls.

7. **Using Technology to Automate Tasks:**

- ○ Leverage technology to automate repetitive tasks, such as scheduling, invoicing, or social media posting. Automation saves time and ensures consistency.

- ○ **Example:** Use automation tools like Zapier to streamline workflows and reduce manual tasks.

Balancing Goals

Strategies for Managing Multiple Goals Simultaneously

Balancing multiple goals can be challenging, but with the right strategies, you can effectively manage and achieve them. Here are some techniques to help you juggle multiple objectives:

1. **Setting Priorities:**

   ○ Clearly define the priority level of each goal. Focus on high-priority goals first, ensuring that you allocate sufficient time and resources to them.

   ○ **Example:** If your top priority is career advancement, prioritize tasks related to professional development over other goals.

2. **Creating a Master Schedule:**

   ○ Develop a master schedule that outlines all your goals and the steps needed to achieve them. This schedule should include specific times for working on each goal, ensuring balanced attention.

   ○ **Example:** Allocate specific days of the week to focus on different goals, such as Mondays for fitness, Tuesdays for career development, and Wednesdays for personal projects.

3. **Using Goal Rotation:**

○ Rotate your focus between different goals to ensure steady progress across all areas. This method prevents burnout and maintains motivation.

○ **Example:** Spend one week focusing intensively on a fitness goal and the next week on a professional goal, rotating regularly to maintain momentum.

4. Integrating Goals:

○ Find ways to integrate your goals, allowing you to work on multiple objectives simultaneously. This can create synergies and make your efforts more efficient.

○ **Example:** Combine your goal of improving fitness with social goals by joining a group exercise class with friends.

5. Regularly Reviewing Progress:

○ Schedule regular reviews to assess your progress on each goal. Adjust your plans and priorities based on these reviews to stay on track.

○ **Example:** Conduct a weekly review every Sunday evening to evaluate your progress and plan the upcoming week.

6. Practicing Flexibility:

○ Be flexible and adaptable in your approach. Life is unpredictable, and being able to adjust your plans as needed is crucial for managing multiple goals.

○ **Example:** If an unexpected work deadline arises, adjust your schedule to accommodate it while ensuring you still make progress on other goals.

7. Maintaining Balance:

○ Strive for balance in your life by setting realistic expectations and avoiding overcommitment. Ensure you allocate time for rest, relaxation, and self-care.

○ **Example:** Set boundaries for work and personal time, ensuring you have time to recharge and avoid burnout.

Example Continuation:

Let's continue with our marathon training example. You might also have career goals and personal development goals. To balance these, you could:

- **Set Priorities:** Determine that marathon training is a high-priority goal for the next six months.

- **Create a Master Schedule:** Allocate specific times each week for training, professional development, and personal projects.

- **Use Goal Rotation:** Focus intensively on training during weekdays and dedicate weekends to personal development activities.

- **Integrate Goals:** Combine socializing with friends and marathon training by inviting them to join your runs.

- **Review Progress:** Conduct weekly reviews to assess your progress in training and adjust your schedule as needed.

- **Practice Flexibility:** Be prepared to adjust your training schedule if work demands increase, while still making time for essential workouts.

- **Maintain Balance:** Ensure you allocate time for rest and relaxation to avoid burnout and maintain overall well-being.

Practical Applications and Studies

Implementing Time Management and Productivity Techniques

1. **Health and Fitness Goals:**

   ○ **Time Management:** Use the Pomodoro Technique for focused workout sessions. Block time in your schedule for regular exercise.

- **Productivity Hacks:** Batch meal preparation to save time during the week. Use fitness apps to track progress and set reminders for workouts.

- **Balancing Goals:** Integrate fitness activities with socializing, like joining a sports club or group fitness class.

2. Career Advancement Goals:

- **Time Management:** Apply time blocking to dedicate specific hours to professional development, networking, and skill-building.

- **Productivity Hacks:** Delegate routine tasks to free up time for high-priority projects. Use automation tools for scheduling and follow-ups.

- **Balancing Goals:** Rotate focus between immediate work tasks and long-term career goals, ensuring balanced progress.

3. Personal Development Goals:

- **Time Management:** Use the GTD method to capture and organize personal development tasks. Set specific times for reading, learning, and practicing new skills.

- **Productivity Hacks:** Eliminate distractions by creating a dedicated learning environment. Use the Two-Minute Rule to quickly address small tasks.

○ **Balancing Goals:** Integrate personal development with other goals, such as learning a new skill related to your profession.

Scientific Studies Supporting Time Management and Productivity

1. Study by Dr. Francesco Cirillo:

○ Dr. Cirillo's research on the Pomodoro Technique demonstrates its effectiveness in maintaining focus and productivity. Breaking work into intervals with breaks helps sustain attention and reduce burnout.

2. Study by Dr. David Allen:

○ Dr. Allen's research on the GTD method highlights the importance of capturing and organizing tasks to reduce mental clutter and improve productivity. His studies show that a structured approach to task management enhances overall efficiency.

3. Study by Dr. Piers Steel:

○ Dr. Steel's research on procrastination identifies key strategies for overcoming procrastination, such as setting specific deadlines and breaking tasks into manageable steps. His findings emphasize the role of self-regulation in achieving goals.

4. **Study by Dr. Carol Dweck:**

- Dr. Dweck's research on growth mindset underscores the importance of viewing challenges as opportunities for growth. Her studies show that individuals with a growth mindset are more likely to persist in the face of obstacles and achieve their goals.

Conclusion

In this chapter, we've explored effective time management strategies, productivity hacks, and techniques for balancing multiple goals. Managing your time efficiently and boosting your productivity are essential skills for achieving your objectives and maintaining balance in your life.

By implementing strategies like the Pomodoro Technique, Eisenhower Matrix, and time blocking, you can optimize your time and focus on high-impact tasks. Productivity hacks such as batching tasks, eliminating distractions, and using automation tools can further enhance your efficiency.

Balancing multiple goals requires clear priorities, a master schedule, and regular reviews. Integrating your goals and maintaining flexibility ensures steady progress across all areas of your life.

As we continue our journey, remember that time management and productivity are ongoing practices. Stay committed to refining your techniques and adapting to new challenges. Let's move forward with confidence, equipped with the tools and strategies to achieve our goals efficiently and effectively.

Stay focused, stay productive, and let's achieve greatness together.

11

ACCOUNTABILITY AND SUPPORT SYSTEMS

In the previous chapters, we explored effective time management strategies and productivity hacks to help you achieve your goals. However, even the most well-crafted plans can benefit from the additional reinforcement of accountability and support systems. This chapter will delve into the role of accountability partners, the importance of a supportive community, and the benefits of joining goal-setting groups. We'll also provide practical advice on how to find and maintain these valuable resources.

Role of Accountability Partners

Finding and Working with Accountability Partners

An accountability partner is someone who supports you in your goal-setting journey by providing motivation, encouragement, and honest feedback. Working with an accountability partner can significantly enhance your chances of success.

1. **Identifying Potential Partners:**

   - Look for individuals who share similar goals, values, or interests. They could be friends, family members, colleagues, or even mentors.

   - **Example:** If your goal is to improve your fitness, consider partnering with a friend who also wants to get in shape or a colleague who enjoys working out.

2. **Setting Clear Expectations:**

   - Establish clear expectations and guidelines for your partnership. Discuss how often you will check in, what type of support you need, and how you will hold each other accountable.

   - **Example:** Agree to weekly check-ins where you both share your progress, challenges, and next steps.

3. **Regular Check-Ins:**

   - Consistent communication is key to maintaining accountability. Schedule regular check-ins to discuss your progress, celebrate successes, and address any obstacles.

○ **Example:** Set up a weekly call or meeting every Sunday evening to review your progress and plan for the upcoming week.

4. Providing Constructive Feedback:

○ Give and receive constructive feedback. Honest, supportive feedback helps you stay on track and identify areas for improvement.

○ **Example:** If your partner is struggling with motivation, offer encouragement and suggest practical solutions based on your own experiences.

5. Celebrating Milestones:

○ Celebrate each other's achievements, no matter how small. Recognizing and celebrating milestones boosts motivation and reinforces your commitment.

○ **Example:** Treat yourselves to a special outing or activity when you reach a significant milestone, such as completing a major project or achieving a fitness goal.

Example Continuation:

Continuing with our marathon training example, you could find an accountability partner who is also training for a marathon. You might agree to run together on certain days, share your weekly progress, and motivate each other to stay committed to your training plans.

Building a Support Network

Importance of a Supportive Community

A supportive community provides encouragement, resources, and a sense of belonging. Surrounding yourself with people who understand and support your goals can significantly enhance your motivation and resilience.

1. **Emotional Support:**

   ○ A supportive community offers emotional support during challenging times. They can provide a listening ear, encouragement, and reassurance.

   ○ **Example:** If you're feeling discouraged about your progress, talking to a supportive friend or family member can help lift your spirits.

2. **Shared Knowledge and Resources:**

   ○ Members of your support network can share valuable knowledge, resources, and experiences that can help you achieve your goals more effectively.

○ **Example:** A colleague who has completed a marathon might share training tips and strategies that worked for them.

3. Accountability:

○ Being part of a community creates a sense of accountability. Knowing that others are aware of your goals and progress can motivate you to stay on track.

○ **Example:** Joining a running group where members regularly share their training updates can encourage you to keep up with your own training.

4. Inspiration and Motivation:

○ Seeing others achieve their goals can inspire and motivate you to pursue your own. Success stories within your community can serve as powerful reminders of what is possible.

○ **Example:** Hearing about a friend's successful weight loss journey can inspire you to stay committed to your fitness goals.

How to Build and Maintain Support Systems

1. Identify Key Individuals:

○ Identify individuals who can provide different types of

support, such as emotional, informational, and practical support. Diversifying your support network ensures you have the right resources for various needs.

- ○ **Example:** Include friends for emotional support, colleagues for professional advice, and mentors for guidance.

2. Communicate Openly:

- ○ Maintain open and honest communication with your support network. Share your goals, progress, challenges, and successes.

- ○ **Example:** Regularly update your support network on your marathon training progress, including any obstacles you encounter.

3. Offer Support in Return:

- ○ A supportive community is reciprocal. Offer your support and encouragement to others in your network, creating a mutually beneficial relationship.

- ○ **Example:** Provide feedback and encouragement to a friend who is working on their own fitness goals.

4. Engage in Community Activities:

- ○ Participate in activities and events that foster a sense of community. Engaging in group activities can strengthen your connections and provide additional motivation.

- **Example:** Join local running events, workshops, or social gatherings related to your goals.

5. Be Consistent:

- Consistency is key to maintaining strong support systems. Regularly engage with your support network and make it a priority to stay connected.

- **Example:** Schedule monthly meetups with your support network to discuss your goals and progress.

Example Continuation:

For marathon training, you might build a support network that includes a running group, a fitness coach, and supportive friends and family. Regularly updating them on your progress, participating in group runs, and offering support in return can help you stay motivated and committed.

Joining Groups and Communities

Benefits of Goal-Setting Groups

Joining goal-setting groups can provide additional structure, accountability, and motivation. These groups bring together individuals with similar objectives, creating a collaborative environment for goal achievement.

1. **Structured Support:**

   ○ Goal-setting groups often have structured meetings, activities, and accountability practices that help members stay focused and on track.

   ○ **Example:** A marathon training group might have scheduled runs, workshops on nutrition and injury prevention, and regular check-ins.

2. **Shared Experiences:**

   ○ Being part of a group allows you to share experiences, challenges, and successes with others who understand your journey. This shared understanding can be incredibly validating and motivating.

   ○ **Example:** Members of a writing group can share their struggles with writer's block and offer solutions that have worked for them.

3. **Access to Expertise:**

   ○ Many goal-setting groups include members with expertise in various areas. Access to this knowledge can help you overcome obstacles and achieve your goals more efficiently.

- **Example:** A fitness group might include personal trainers or nutritionists who can offer professional advice.

4. Increased Accountability:

- Group settings naturally create a sense of accountability, as you are more likely to stay committed to your goals when others are aware of your progress.

- **Example:** Knowing that you have to report your weekly training progress to your running group can motivate you to stick to your schedule.

5. Motivation and Encouragement:

- The collective motivation and encouragement from a group can boost your morale and keep you moving forward, especially during challenging times.

- **Example:** A goal-setting group might celebrate each member's milestones, providing positive reinforcement that encourages continued effort.

How to Find and Join Relevant Groups

1. Identify Your Goals and Interests:

○ Determine what specific goals or interests you want to focus on. This clarity will help you find groups that align with your objectives.

○ **Example:** If your goal is to improve your public speaking skills, look for groups focused on communication and presentation skills.

2. Research and Explore:

○ Use online platforms, social media, and local community resources to find groups related to your goals. Websites like Meetup, Facebook, and LinkedIn offer numerous groups and communities.

○ **Example:** Search for marathon training groups on Meetup or join a fitness community on Facebook.

3. Attend Meetings and Events:

○ Attend initial meetings or events to get a sense of the group's dynamics and activities. This helps you determine if the group is a good fit for you.

○ **Example:** Attend a few sessions of a local writing group to see if their approach and members resonate with your goals.

4. Engage Actively:

○ Actively participate in group activities, discussions, and events. Engagement fosters connections and helps you fully benefit from the group's support.

○ **Example:** Contribute to discussions in a professional development group by sharing your experiences and insights.

5. **Evaluate and Commit:**

○ After attending a few sessions, evaluate the group's impact on your progress. If you find it beneficial, commit to regular participation.

○ **Example:** If you feel motivated and supported by your running group, commit to attending their weekly runs and workshops.

Example Continuation:

For marathon training, you could join a local running club that offers group runs, training plans, and expert advice. Actively participating in the club's activities and engaging with fellow members can provide the support and accountability you need to stay on track.

Practical Applications and Studies

Implementing Accountability and Support Techniques

1. **Health and Fitness Goals:**

   ○ **Accountability Partners:** Find a workout buddy who shares your fitness goals. Regular check-ins and joint workouts can keep you motivated.

   ○ **Support Network:** Join a fitness community or online forum where members share their progress and support each other.

   ○ **Goal-Setting Groups:** Participate in a local running club or fitness challenge group for structured support and accountability.

2. **Career Advancement Goals:**

   ○ **Accountability Partners:** Partner with a colleague or mentor who can provide guidance and hold you accountable for your career development goals.

   ○ **Support Network:** Build a professional network through industry associations and LinkedIn groups.

   ○ **Goal-Setting Groups:** Join a professional development group or mastermind group to gain insights and support from peers.

3. **Personal Development Goals:**

- **Accountability Partners:** Find a friend or family member who shares your interest in personal growth. Regular discussions and check-ins can keep you on track.

- **Support Network:** Engage with online communities or local groups focused on personal development topics such as mindfulness or public speaking.

- **Goal-Setting Groups:** Participate in workshops or classes that provide structure and support for your personal development journey.

Scientific Studies Supporting Accountability and Support Systems

1. Study by Dr. Gail Matthews:

- Dr. Matthews' research at the Dominican University of California found that individuals who shared their goals with a friend and maintained accountability through regular updates were significantly more likely to achieve their goals.

2. Study by Dr. David McClelland:

- Dr. McClelland's research on the influence of social networks highlights the importance of surrounding yourself with high-achieving, supportive individuals.

His studies show that having a positive support net-work can enhance goal achievement.

3. **Study by Dr. Julianne Holt-Lunstad:**

○ Dr. Holt-Lunstad's research on social relationships and health demonstrates that strong social connections improve overall well-being and resilience, which are crucial for goal achievement.

Conclusion

In this chapter, we've explored the vital role of accountability part-ners, the importance of a supportive community, and the benefits of joining goal-setting groups. Building and maintaining these support systems can significantly enhance your ability to achieve your goals by providing motivation, encouragement, and valuable resources.

Accountability partners offer personalized support and feedback, helping you stay committed to your goals. A supportive commu-nity provides emotional backing, shared knowledge, and a sense of belonging. Joining goal-setting groups adds structure, account-ability, and collective motivation to your journey.

As we continue our journey, remember that achieving your goals is not a solitary endeavor. Leveraging the power of accountability and support systems can transform your goal-setting process and lead to greater success. Let's move forward with confidence, knowing that we have a strong network of support to help us achieve greatness together.

Stay connected, stay supported, and let's achieve our goals with the power of accountability and community.

12

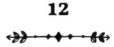

REVIEWING AND ADJUSTING GOALS

In the previous chapters, we've discussed the critical roles of accountability and support systems in achieving your goals. Now, let's focus on the importance of regular goal reviews and the process of adjusting goals based on your progress and changing circumstances. We will also explore the significance of celebrating milestones and reflecting on your achievements. This chapter will provide you with the techniques and insights necessary to ensure your goal-setting process remains dynamic and responsive.

Regular Reviews

Importance of Regular Goal Reviews

Regularly reviewing your goals is essential to ensure that you stay on track and make necessary adjustments. This practice helps you to stay focused, motivated, and aligned with your long-term objectives. Without regular reviews, it's easy to lose sight of your goals and become overwhelmed by daily tasks.

1. **Maintaining Focus:**

   - Regular reviews help you maintain focus on your priorities by reminding you of your goals and the reasons behind them. This ongoing attention prevents you from getting sidetracked.

   - **Example:** If you're training for a marathon, a weekly review of your training schedule ensures you stay committed and adjust your plan based on your progress.

2. **Assessing Progress:**

   - Reviews provide an opportunity to assess your progress and identify what is working and what isn't. This evaluation helps you make informed decisions about any changes needed.

   - **Example:** If you notice during your review that you're consistently struggling with long runs, you might need to adjust your training plan or seek additional support.

3. Identifying Challenges:

- Regular reviews allow you to identify challenges and obstacles early on. Addressing these issues promptly can prevent them from derailing your progress.

- **Example:** If you're falling behind on a work project, a review can help you pinpoint the cause and implement strategies to get back on track.

4. Staying Motivated:

- Reflecting on your achievements and recognizing your progress can boost your motivation. Regularly seeing how far you've come reinforces your commitment.

- **Example:** Celebrating small wins in your marathon training, such as achieving a new personal best, can keep you motivated for the next phase of training.

Techniques for Effective Reviews

1. Weekly Reviews:

- Set aside time each week to review your goals. Assess your progress, identify any obstacles, and plan the upcoming week's activities.

- **Example:** Every Sunday evening, spend 30 minutes reviewing your marathon training log, noting your achievements and planning the next week's workouts.

2. **Monthly Reviews:**

- Conduct a more in-depth review at the end of each month. Evaluate your overall progress, reflect on significant achievements, and make any necessary adjustments to your plan.

- **Example:** At the end of each month, review your fitness progress, adjust your training plan based on your performance, and set new goals for the following month.

3. **Quarterly Reviews:**

- A quarterly review allows you to step back and assess your long-term progress. This is an opportunity to evaluate your goals and ensure they still align with your overall vision.

- **Example:** Every three months, review your career development goals, assess your progress, and adjust your strategies as needed.

4. **Annual Reviews:**

- An annual review is a comprehensive evaluation of your goals and achievements over the past year. Reflect on what worked, what didn't, and set new goals for the coming year.

- ○ **Example:** At the end of the year, review your overall marathon training journey, celebrate your successes, and set new fitness goals for the next year.

5. Journaling:

- ○ Keep a journal to document your thoughts, progress, and reflections during your reviews. Writing down your experiences can provide valuable insights and help you stay accountable.

- ○ **Example:** Maintain a training journal where you record your daily workouts, feelings, and any adjustments made to your training plan.

Example Continuation:

Continuing with our marathon training example, conducting weekly reviews allows you to track your progress and make necessary adjustments to your training plan. Monthly and quarterly reviews provide a broader perspective on your journey, helping you stay motivated and aligned with your long-term goals.

Adapting Goals

How to Adjust Goals Based on Progress and Changes

As you progress towards your goals, it's essential to remain flexible and adapt to new circumstances. Adjusting your goals ensures they remain relevant and achievable despite any changes or challenges you encounter.

1. **Evaluating Feasibility:**

   ○ Regularly assess whether your goals are still feasible based on your current situation. If circumstances have changed, adjust your goals to reflect new realities.

   ○ **Example:** If you experience an injury during marathon training, adjust your goal to allow for adequate recovery time while still maintaining progress.

2. **Modifying Strategies:**

   ○ If your current strategies are not yielding the desired results, be open to trying new approaches. Adjusting your strategies can help you overcome obstacles and stay on track.

   ○ **Example:** If you find your current training routine too strenuous, consider incorporating more cross-training or rest days to prevent burnout.

3. **Setting New Milestones:**

   ○ Break down your goals into smaller, more manageable milestones. Adjust these milestones as needed to maintain a sense of progress and achievement.

○ **Example:** If completing a marathon seems over-whelming, set intermediate milestones like completing a 10K or half-marathon first.

4. Seeking Feedback:

○ Seek feedback from mentors, accountability partners, or support groups. External perspectives can provide valuable insights and help you refine your goals and strategies.

○ **Example:** Discuss your training progress with a coach or experienced runner to gain insights and advice on improving your performance.

5. Staying Flexible:

○ Embrace a flexible mindset that allows for adjustments without feeling discouraged. Understand that setbacks are part of the journey and use them as learning opportunities.

○ **Example:** If you need to adjust your goal timeline due to unforeseen circumstances, recognize that it's a strategic decision to ensure long-term success.

Example Continuation:

In the context of marathon training, adapting your goals might involve adjusting your training intensity, seeking alternative training methods, or setting new milestones to accommodate any changes in your schedule or physical condition. Flexibility and a willingness to adapt are crucial for maintaining progress and achieving your ultimate goal.

Celebrating Wins

Importance of Celebrating Milestones

Celebrating milestones and reflecting on your achievements is an essential part of the goal-setting process. Recognizing your progress boosts motivation, reinforces positive behavior, and provides a sense of accomplishment.

1. **Boosting Motivation:**

   - Celebrating milestones provides positive reinforcement, boosting your motivation to continue working towards your goals.

   - **Example:** Reward yourself with a special treat or activity after reaching a significant training milestone, such as completing a long run.

2. **Reinforcing Positive Behavior:**

○ Acknowledging your achievements reinforces the behaviors and strategies that led to success. This positive reinforcement encourages you to continue using effective approaches.

○ **Example:** If cross-training contributed to your progress, celebrate that success and make cross-training a regular part of your routine.

3. Providing a Sense of Accomplishment:

○ Celebrating milestones gives you a tangible sense of accomplishment, reminding you that your efforts are paying off.

○ **Example:** Displaying your race medals or keeping a visual record of your achievements can provide ongoing motivation and pride.

4. Enhancing Well-Being:

○ Celebrating successes contributes to overall well-being by fostering positive emotions and reducing stress.

○ **Example:** Taking time to celebrate with friends and family can strengthen relationships and enhance your sense of community and support.

Methods to Celebrate and Reflect on Achievements

1. **Personal Rewards:**

   ○ Treat yourself to something special that you enjoy, such as a favorite meal, a new book, or a relaxing spa day.

   ○ **Example:** After completing a particularly challenging training week, reward yourself with a massage to help your muscles recover.

2. **Public Recognition:**

   ○ Share your achievements with your support network. Public recognition can provide additional encouragement and motivation.

   ○ **Example:** Post about your progress on social media or share your accomplishments with your running group.

3. **Reflection Journals:**

   ○ Maintain a reflection journal where you document your achievements, the strategies that worked, and any lessons learned. Reflecting on your journey helps solidify your progress and plan for future goals.

   ○ **Example:** Write about your feelings and experiences after completing a race, noting what contributed to your success and any areas for improvement.

4. Celebration Events:

○ Organize a celebration event with friends, family, or colleagues to mark significant milestones. Celebrating with others can enhance the joy and sense of accomplishment.

○ **Example:** Host a post-race celebration party to share your achievement with those who supported you along the way.

5. Visual Reminders:

○ Create visual reminders of your achievements, such as a vision board, a progress chart, or displaying medals and certificates. Visual reminders keep your successes in sight and maintain motivation.

○ **Example:** Create a photo collage of your marathon training journey and display it where you can see it daily.

6. Personal Reflection:

○ Take time for personal reflection to acknowledge your hard work and dedication. Reflecting on your journey can deepen your appreciation for your efforts and reinforce your commitment to future goals.

○ **Example:** Spend an evening reflecting on your

progress, perhaps during a quiet walk or meditation session, to internalize your achievements.

Example Continuation:

For marathon training, celebrating wins could involve treating yourself to a new pair of running shoes after reaching a training milestone, sharing your progress with your running group, and hosting a celebration event with friends and family after completing the marathon.

Practical Applications and Studies

Implementing Review and Adjustment Techniques

1. **Health and Fitness Goals:**

   - **Regular Reviews:** Conduct weekly and monthly reviews of your fitness progress. Adjust your workout routine based on your performance and any challenges encountered.

   - **Adapting Goals:** If you experience an injury, adjust your fitness goals to focus on recovery and alternative exercises.

   - **Celebrating Wins:** Celebrate milestones like completing a race or reaching a new personal best by rewarding yourself with new fitness gear or a relaxing day off.

2. Career Advancement Goals:

- **Regular Reviews:** Schedule quarterly reviews of your career development plan. Assess your progress, seek feedback from mentors, and adjust your strategies as needed.

- **Adapting Goals:** If your job role changes, adjust your career goals to align with your new responsibilities and opportunities.

- **Celebrating Wins:** Celebrate professional achievements such as promotions or successful projects by sharing your success with colleagues and treating yourself to a special reward.

3. Personal Development Goals:

- **Regular Reviews:** Maintain a reflection journal where you regularly review your personal development goals and progress.

- **Adapting Goals:** If your interests or priorities change, adjust your personal development goals to reflect your new direction.

- **Celebrating Wins:** Celebrate achievements like

completing a course or mastering a new skill by sharing your success with friends and rewarding yourself with a meaningful experience.

Scientific Studies Supporting Regular Reviews and Celebrations

1. **Study by Dr. Gail Matthews:**

   - Dr. Matthews' research at the Dominican University of California found that individuals who wrote down their goals, shared them with others, and regularly reviewed their progress were significantly more likely to achieve their goals.

2. **Study by Dr. Teresa Amabile:**

   - Dr. Amabile's research on the progress principle highlights the importance of celebrating small wins. Her studies show that recognizing and celebrating progress boosts motivation and overall performance.

3. **Study by Dr. Edwin Locke:**

   - Dr. Locke's goal-setting theory emphasizes the importance of specific, challenging goals and regular feedback. His research shows that regular reviews and adjustments lead to higher goal achievement.

4. **Study by Dr. Martin Seligman:**

◦ Dr. Seligman's research on positive psychology and well-being demonstrates that celebrating achievements and reflecting on positive experiences enhances overall happiness and motivation.

Conclusion

In this chapter, we've explored the importance of regular goal reviews, adapting goals based on progress and changes, and celebrating milestones. These practices ensure that your goal-setting process remains dynamic, responsive, and motivating.

Regular reviews help you maintain focus, assess progress, and address challenges promptly. Adapting your goals as needed ensures they remain relevant and achievable despite changing circumstances. Celebrating milestones reinforces positive behavior, boosts motivation, and provides a sense of accomplishment.

By implementing these techniques, you can maintain momentum and stay committed to your goals. Remember that goal achievement is a journey that requires flexibility, reflection, and celebration. Let's continue our journey with confidence, equipped with the tools and strategies to achieve our goals and celebrate our successes.

Stay focused, stay adaptable, and let's achieve greatness together.

PART 4

Success Stories

13

PERSONAL GOALS ACHIEVED

In the previous chapters, we discussed the importance of regular reviews, adapting goals based on progress, and celebrating milestones. Now, let's explore the inspiring stories of individuals who have achieved their personal goals. These detailed stories will provide key takeaways and practical advice, demonstrating how the principles we've discussed can be applied in real-life situations. Through these success stories, you will see the power of perseverance, resilience, and effective goal-setting.

Inspirational Stories

Story 1: Sarah's Journey to Health and Fitness

Background: Sarah, a 35-year-old mother of two, had always struggled with her weight. After her second child, she found it increasingly difficult to lose the extra pounds. Her busy schedule as a working mom left her with little time for exercise or meal planning.

Goals: Sarah set a goal to lose 50 pounds within a year and improve her overall fitness. She aimed to run a 5K race by the end of the year as a milestone.

Challenges:

- Limited time due to work and family responsibilities

- Lack of knowledge about proper nutrition and exercise

- Initial lack of motivation and self-confidence

Strategies:

1. Setting SMART Goals:

- Sarah set specific, measurable, achievable, relevant, and time-bound goals. She broke down her weight loss goal into monthly targets and created a detailed plan for achieving them.

2. Finding an Accountability Partner:

- She partnered with her friend Lisa, who also wanted to get fit. They committed to weekly check-ins and supported each other through the journey.

3. Joining a Support Group:

- ○ Sarah joined an online fitness community where members shared their progress, challenges, and tips. This group provided motivation and practical advice.

4. Regular Reviews and Adjustments:

- ○ She conducted weekly reviews to assess her progress and made adjustments to her diet and exercise routine as needed.

5. Celebrating Milestones:

- ○ Sarah celebrated small victories, such as losing her first 10 pounds and completing her first 5K run. These celebrations boosted her motivation and reinforced her commitment.

Results: By the end of the year, Sarah had lost 52 pounds, surpassing her initial goal. She completed her first 5K race and even set a new goal to run a half-marathon. Her journey transformed her physically and mentally, boosting her confidence and overall well-being.

Lessons Learned:

- • Setting clear, achievable goals and breaking them into

smaller milestones is crucial for maintaining motivation.

- Finding an accountability partner and joining a supportive community can provide essential encouragement and resources.

- Regular reviews and adjustments help to stay on track and adapt to changing circumstances.

- Celebrating milestones reinforces positive behavior and keeps motivation high.

Studies Supporting Sarah's Success:

- Dr. Gail Matthews' research on the effectiveness of writing down goals and having accountability partners highlights the importance of Sarah's approach.

- Dr. Teresa Amabile's progress principle underscores the significance of celebrating small wins, which played a crucial role in Sarah's journey.

Story 2: John's Professional Transformation

Background: John, a 45-year-old marketing manager, felt stagnant in his career. He had been in the same position for over a decade and wanted to advance to a senior management role. However, he lacked certain skills and felt overwhelmed by the prospect of returning to study and balancing work and family life.

Goals: John aimed to earn an advanced certification in digital marketing within two years and secure a senior management position within three years.

Challenges:

- Balancing work, studies, and family commitments

- Overcoming the fear of returning to formal education after many years

- Keeping up with the fast-paced changes in digital marketing

Strategies:

1. **Creating a Detailed Action Plan:**

   ○ John outlined the steps needed to achieve his certification, including enrolling in courses, scheduling study time, and setting deadlines for completing coursework.

2. Time Management Techniques:

- He used time blocking to allocate specific times for studying, work, and family. This helped him manage his responsibilities without feeling overwhelmed.

3. Seeking Support:

- John discussed his goals with his family and employer, gaining their support. His employer agreed to provide flexible work hours to accommodate his studies.

4. Joining a Study Group:

- He joined a study group with fellow professionals pursuing the same certification. This group provided motivation, shared resources, and a platform for discussing challenges.

5. Regular Reviews and Feedback:

- John conducted monthly reviews of his progress and sought feedback from his study group and mentors to improve his performance.

6. Celebrating Achievements:

- He celebrated each completed course and passing exam, treating himself to small rewards and acknowledging his hard work.

Results: John successfully earned his digital marketing certification within 18 months. Shortly after, he was promoted to a senior management position in his company. His proactive approach to learning and career development paid off, leading to significant professional growth and increased job satisfaction.

Lessons Learned:

- A detailed action plan with clear deadlines is essential for managing complex goals.

- Effective time management techniques, such as time blocking, can help balance multiple responsibilities.

- Seeking support from family, employers, and peers can provide the necessary resources and motivation.

- Regular reviews and feedback are crucial for continuous improvement.

- Celebrating achievements helps maintain motivation and acknowledges hard work.

Studies Supporting John's Success:

- Dr. David Allen's Getting Things Done (GTD) methodology supports the importance of a structured approach to managing tasks and time.

- Dr. Edwin Locke's goal-setting theory highlights the benefits of setting specific, challenging goals and seeking regular feedback.

Story 3: Emily's Personal Development Journey

Background: Emily, a 28-year-old graphic designer, felt unfulfilled in her career and personal life. She had always dreamed of becoming a writer but lacked the confidence to pursue her passion. Emily decided to set personal development goals to improve her skills and confidence.

Goals: Emily set a goal to write and publish her first book within two years. She also aimed to develop her public speaking skills to promote her book and build her personal brand.

Challenges:

- Overcoming self-doubt and fear of failure

- Finding time to write while working full-time

- Developing public speaking skills from scratch

Strategies:

1. **Setting Incremental Goals:**

   ○ Emily broke down her goal into smaller, manageable tasks, such as writing a chapter each month and attending weekly writing workshops.

2. **Creating a Support System:**

   ○ She joined a local writers' group where members

shared their work, provided feedback, and supported each other's progress.

3. Regular Practice and Improvement:

- ○ Emily dedicated time each day to writing and enrolled in public speaking courses to build her confidence and skills.

4. Seeking Mentorship:

- ○ She sought mentorship from a published author who provided guidance, feedback, and encouragement throughout her writing journey.

5. Regular Reviews and Adjustments:

- ○ Emily conducted bi-weekly reviews of her writing progress and made adjustments to her schedule and approach based on feedback and self-reflection.

6. Celebrating Milestones:

- ○ She celebrated each completed chapter and public speaking engagement, rewarding herself with activities she enjoyed.

Results: Emily completed her book within 18 months and successfully published it. She also became a confident public speaker, promoting her book at various events and building a strong personal brand. Her journey of personal development transformed her life, allowing her to pursue her passion and achieve her dreams.

Lessons Learned:

- Setting incremental goals makes large objectives more manageable and less overwhelming.

- Building a support system and seeking mentorship provide valuable guidance and encouragement.

- Regular practice and continuous improvement are essential for developing new skills.

- Conducting regular reviews and making necessary adjustments help maintain progress.

- Celebrating milestones reinforces positive behavior and boosts motivation.

Studies Supporting Emily's Success:

- Dr. Carol Dweck's research on growth mindset emphasizes the importance of viewing challenges as opportunities for growth.

- Dr. Angela Duckworth's studies on grit highlight the role of perseverance and passion in achieving long-term goals.

Practical Applications and Studies

Implementing Success Strategies in Your Own Goals

1. **Health and Fitness Goals:**

   ○ **Setting SMART Goals:** Define clear and achievable fitness goals with specific timelines.

   ○ **Building a Support Network:** Join fitness groups or online communities for motivation and support.

   ○ **Regular Reviews and Adjustments:** Conduct weekly reviews to track progress and adjust your workout routine as needed.

   ○ **Celebrating Wins:** Celebrate milestones like weight loss or improved fitness levels with personal rewards.

2. **Career Advancement Goals:**

   ○ **Creating a Detailed Action Plan:** Outline the steps needed to achieve your career goals, including additional training or certifications.

   ○ **Time Management Techniques:** Use time blocking and prioritize tasks to balance work and personal development.

   ○ **Seeking Support:** Discuss your goals with your employer and seek mentorship from experienced professionals.

- ○ **Celebrating Achievements:** Acknowledge your professional accomplishments and reward yourself for hard work.

3. Personal Development Goals:

- ○ **Setting Incremental Goals:** Break down large personal development goals into smaller, manageable tasks.

- ○ **Joining Support Groups:** Participate in groups or classes focused on your personal development interests.

- ○ **Regular Practice and Improvement:** Dedicate consistent time to practice and refine your skills.

- ○ **Celebrating Milestones:** Recognize and celebrate each step forward in your personal development journey.

Scientific Studies Supporting Goal Achievement:

1. Study by Dr. Gail Matthews:

- ○ Dr. Matthews' research emphasizes the effectiveness of writing down goals and having accountability partners. Her findings highlight the increased likelihood of achieving goals through structured planning and support.

2. **Study by Dr. Carol Dweck:**

○ Dr. Dweck's research on growth mindset underscores the importance of viewing challenges as learning opportunities. Her studies show that individuals with a growth mindset are more resilient and better equipped to achieve their goals.

3. **Study by Dr. Angela Duckworth:**

○ Dr. Duckworth's research on grit reveals that perseverance and passion are critical for long-term success. Her studies demonstrate that sustained effort over time leads to significant achievements.

Conclusion

In this chapter, we've explored inspiring stories of individuals who achieved their personal goals through perseverance, effective goal-setting, and the support of their networks. These success stories provide valuable lessons and practical advice that you can apply to your own goals.

By setting clear, achievable goals, building strong support systems, regularly reviewing progress, and celebrating milestones, you can enhance your motivation and commitment. The strategies and insights from these stories, supported by scientific research, offer a roadmap for achieving your own personal goals.

As we continue our journey, remember that success is not a destination but a continuous process of growth and improvement. Stay inspired by the stories of others, apply the lessons learned, and keep striving towards your dreams. Together, we can achieve greatness.

Stay motivated, stay resilient, and let's achieve our personal goals with the power of effective goal-setting and supportive communities.

14

❖❖ ⋯ ❖◆❖ ⋯ ❖❖

PROFESSIONAL GOALS ACHIEVED

In the previous chapter, we explored inspiring stories of individuals who achieved their personal goals. Now, let's shift our focus to professional goals and business success. This chapter will highlight examples of professional goal achievement, providing key insights and strategies from successful individuals. These stories will demonstrate how effective goal-setting, perseverance, and the right support systems can lead to remarkable career and business accomplishments.

Career and Business Success

Story 1: Emma's Journey to Executive Leadership

Background: Emma, a marketing manager in her mid-thirties, aspired to climb the corporate ladder and attain an executive leadership position within her company. Despite her strong performance and dedication, she felt that her career growth had stagnated.

Goals: Emma set a goal to become the Director of Marketing within three years and eventually aim for a C-suite position within five years.

Challenges:

- Limited leadership experience

- Balancing professional development with current job responsibilities

- Navigating a competitive corporate environment

Strategies:

1. **Creating a Professional Development Plan:**

   - Emma outlined a detailed plan that included gaining leadership experience, improving her skills, and expanding her professional network. She identified key milestones and deadlines for achieving each step.

2. **Seeking Mentorship:**

   - She sought mentorship from a senior executive within her company. This mentor provided guidance, feedback, and support, helping Emma navigate her career path more effectively.

3. Investing in Education:

- Emma enrolled in an executive leadership program to enhance her skills and credentials. She balanced her studies with her work by managing her time effectively and prioritizing tasks.

4. Taking on Challenging Projects:

- She volunteered for high-visibility projects that showcased her abilities and provided valuable leadership experience. These projects also helped her build a strong reputation within the company.

5. Building a Professional Network:

- Emma actively participated in industry events, conferences, and networking groups. This expanded her connections and opened up new opportunities for career advancement.

6. Regular Reviews and Adjustments:

- She conducted quarterly reviews of her progress, sought feedback from her mentor, and adjusted her strategies as needed to stay on track.

7. **Celebrating Achievements:**

  ○ Emma celebrated her professional milestones, such as completing the leadership program and successfully leading major projects. These celebrations boosted her motivation and reinforced her commitment.

Results: Within three years, Emma was promoted to the Director of Marketing. Her proactive approach to professional development, coupled with the support of her mentor and network, played a crucial role in her success. She continued to set new goals and work towards a C-suite position, confident in her ability to achieve her aspirations.

Lessons Learned:

- A detailed professional development plan with clear milestones and deadlines is essential for career advancement.

- Seeking mentorship provides valuable guidance and support.

- Investing in education and skill development enhances qualifications and confidence.

- Taking on challenging projects showcases abilities and builds a strong professional reputation.

- Building a professional network opens up new opportunities and resources.

- Regular reviews and adjustments ensure continuous progress.

- Celebrating achievements boosts motivation and reinforces commitment.

Studies Supporting Emma's Success:

- Dr. David Clutterbuck's research on mentorship emphasizes the benefits of having a mentor for career development and achieving professional goals.

- Dr. Carol Dweck's growth mindset theory supports the importance of continuous learning and embracing challenges for career advancement.

Story 2: Michael's Entrepreneurial Success

Background: Michael, a software engineer in his early forties, had always dreamed of starting his own tech company. Despite his technical skills and industry knowledge, he hesitated to take the plunge due to the risks and uncertainties involved in entrepreneurship.

Goals: Michael set a goal to launch his tech startup within one year and achieve a profitable business within three years.

Challenges:

- Limited experience in business management and entrepreneurship

- Financial risks and securing funding

- Building a team and developing a marketable product

Strategies:

1. **Conducting Market Research:**

    ○ Michael conducted extensive market research to identify a viable business idea and understand the competitive landscape. He focused on solving a specific problem that had strong demand.

2. **Creating a Business Plan:**

◦ He developed a comprehensive business plan outlining his vision, goals, strategies, financial projections, and marketing plans. This plan served as a roadmap for launching and growing his startup.

3. Seeking Funding:

◦ Michael explored various funding options, including angel investors, venture capital, and crowdfunding. He prepared a compelling pitch and secured initial funding to kickstart his business.

4. Building a Team:

◦ He assembled a team of skilled professionals who shared his vision and were committed to the company's success. Michael focused on hiring individuals with complementary skills and expertise.

5. Developing a Minimum Viable Product (MVP):

◦ Michael's team developed an MVP to test the market and gather feedback. This approach allowed them to refine the product based on real user input and minimize risks.

6. Networking and Partnerships:

◦ He leveraged his professional network to establish partnerships, gain industry insights, and access re-

sources. Networking helped him navigate the entrepreneurial landscape more effectively.

7. **Regular Reviews and Adjustments:**

- Michael conducted monthly reviews of his business
  progress, assessing financial performance, product development, and market response. He made necessary
  adjustments to his strategies based on these reviews.

8. **Celebrating Milestones:**

- He celebrated key milestones, such as launching the
  MVP, securing funding, and achieving initial sales targets. These celebrations motivated his team and reinforced their commitment to the company's vision.

Results: Within a year, Michael successfully launched his tech
startup. His company achieved profitability within three years,
thanks to his strategic planning, effective execution, and the support of his team and network. Michael's entrepreneurial journey
transformed his professional life, fulfilling his dream of building a
successful business.

Lessons Learned:

- Conducting thorough market research is essential for
  identifying viable business opportunities.

- A detailed business plan provides a clear roadmap for

launching and growing a startup.

- Securing funding and managing financial risks are critical for entrepreneurial success.

- Building a strong team with complementary skills is key to developing a successful product.

- Developing an MVP and gathering user feedback minimizes risks and enhances product development.

- Networking and partnerships provide valuable resources and insights.

- Regular reviews and adjustments ensure continuous improvement and growth.

- Celebrating milestones boosts motivation and reinforces the team's commitment.

Studies Supporting Michael's Success:

- Dr. Saras Sarasvathy's research on effectuation in entrepreneurship emphasizes the importance of leveraging available resources and partnerships in building successful startups.

- Dr. Eric Ries' Lean Startup methodology supports the concept of developing an MVP and iterating based on user feedback.

Story 3: Rachel's Freelance Career Growth

Background: Rachel, a graphic designer in her late twenties, worked for a design agency but felt constrained by the lack of creative freedom. She aspired to transition to a full-time freelance career, offering her design services independently.

Goals: Rachel aimed to establish a successful freelance business within two years, with a steady stream of clients and a sustainable income.

Challenges:

- Building a client base from scratch

- Managing the business aspects of freelancing, such as marketing, finances, and client relationships

- Maintaining a work-life balance

Strategies:

1. **Developing a Personal Brand:**

    ○ Rachel created a personal brand that reflected her unique style and expertise. She designed a professional website and portfolio to showcase her work and attract potential clients.

2. **Networking and Marketing:**

○ She actively networked within the design community and utilized social media to market her services. Rachel attended industry events, joined online groups, and participated in forums to build her presence.

3. Offering Value to Clients:

○ Rachel focused on providing exceptional value to her clients by delivering high-quality work, meeting deadlines, and offering excellent customer service. She built strong relationships with her clients, leading to repeat business and referrals.

4. Time Management and Organization:

○ She implemented time management techniques, such as time blocking and task prioritization, to balance her workload and maintain productivity. Rachel used project management tools to stay organized and meet deadlines.

5. Continuous Learning:

○ Rachel invested in continuous learning by taking courses, attending workshops, and staying updated with industry trends. This helped her enhance her skills and offer cutting-edge design solutions to her clients.

6. **Regular Reviews and Adjustments:**

- ○ She conducted monthly reviews of her business performance, assessing client feedback, financial metrics, and workload. Rachel made necessary adjustments to her strategies based on these reviews.

7. **Celebrating Successes:**

- ○ Rachel celebrated her successes, such as securing a major client or completing a challenging project. These celebrations boosted her confidence and motivation.

Results: Within two years, Rachel established a thriving freelance business with a steady stream of clients and a sustainable income. Her creative freedom and business success brought her immense satisfaction and fulfillment.

Lessons Learned:

- Developing a strong personal brand and professional portfolio attracts potential clients.

- Networking and marketing are crucial for building a client base and establishing a presence in the industry.

- Providing exceptional value and building strong client relationships lead to repeat business and referrals.

- Effective time management and organization enhance

productivity and work-life balance.

- Continuous learning and staying updated with industry trends ensure competitiveness and innovation.

- Regular reviews and adjustments help maintain business growth and client satisfaction.

- Celebrating successes boosts confidence and motivation.

Studies Supporting Rachel's Success:

- Dr. Ivan Misner's research on networking highlights the importance of building professional relationships for business growth.

- Dr. Teresa Amabile's research on creativity and productivity emphasizes the value of continuous learning and innovation in creative professions.

Practical Applications and Studies

Implementing Professional Success Strategies in Your Career

1. **Career Advancement Goals:**

   ○ **Creating a Professional Development Plan:** Outline steps for career growth, including gaining new skills, seeking mentorship, and expanding your network.

- **Investing in Education:** Enroll in courses or certifications to enhance your qualifications.

- **Regular Reviews and Adjustments:** Conduct quarterly reviews of your career progress and adjust your strategies as needed.

- **Celebrating Achievements:** Recognize and celebrate professional milestones, such as promotions or completing a major project.

2. Entrepreneurial Goals:

- **Conducting Market Research:** Identify viable business opportunities through thorough research.

- **Creating a Business Plan:** Develop a detailed plan outlining your vision, goals, and strategies.

- **Building a Team:** Assemble a team with complementary skills to support your business growth.

- **Regular Reviews and Adjustments:** Monitor your business performance and make necessary adjustments.

- **Celebrating Milestones:** Celebrate key business milestones, such as launching a product or achieving profitability.

3. Freelance and Independent Business Goals:

- **Developing a Personal Brand:** Create a strong personal brand and professional portfolio.

- **Networking and Marketing:** Actively network and market your services to build a client base.

- **Providing Value to Clients:** Focus on delivering high-quality work and building strong client relationships.

- **Regular Reviews and Adjustments:** Conduct regular reviews of your business performance and client feedback.

- **Celebrating Successes:** Acknowledge and celebrate your successes to boost motivation and confidence.

Scientific Studies Supporting Professional Success:

1. Study by Dr. David Clutterbuck:

- Dr. Clutterbuck's research on mentorship highlights its benefits for career development and achieving professional goals. Mentorship provides valuable guidance, support, and networking opportunities.

2. Study by Dr. Saras Sarasvathy:

- Dr. Sarasvathy's research on effectuation in entrepreneurship emphasizes leveraging available resources and partnerships to build successful startups. This approach reduces risks and enhances business growth.

3. Study by Dr. Ivan Misner:

- Dr. Misner's research on networking demonstrates the importance of building professional relationships for business growth and career advancement. Effective networking leads to new opportunities and valuable resources.

4. Study by Dr. Teresa Amabile:

- Dr. Amabile's research on creativity and productivity highlights the importance of continuous learning and innovation in achieving success in creative professions. Staying updated with industry trends and enhancing skills are crucial for competitiveness.

Conclusion

In this chapter, we've explored inspiring stories of individuals who achieved their professional goals through effective goal-setting, perseverance, and the support of their networks. These success stories provide valuable lessons and practical advice that you can apply to your own career and business goals.

By creating detailed plans, seeking mentorship, investing in education, building strong networks, and regularly reviewing and adjusting strategies, you can enhance your professional growth and achieve remarkable success. Celebrating your achievements reinforces positive behavior and boosts motivation.

As we continue our journey, remember that professional success is a continuous process of growth, learning, and adaptation. Stay inspired by the stories of others, apply the lessons learned, and keep striving towards your career and business aspirations. Together, we can achieve greatness.

Stay focused, stay motivated, and let's achieve our professional goals with the power of effective goal-setting and supportive communities.

15

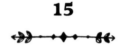

OVERCOMING ADVERSITY

In the previous chapters, we've delved into professional goal achievement and the strategies that drive success. However, the journey to achieving goals is often fraught with challenges and obstacles. In this chapter, we'll explore inspiring stories of individuals who overcame significant adversity to reach their goals. These stories highlight the techniques used to stay focused and motivated despite the odds. By understanding their resilience, you can draw strength and insight to overcome your own challenges.

Stories of Resilience

Story 1: Helen's Triumph Over Health Challenges

Background: Helen, a 50-year-old school teacher, was diagnosed with a severe autoimmune disease that significantly impacted her mobility and energy levels. Despite her condition, Helen was determined to continue her career and achieve her goal of earning a Master's degree in Education.

Goals: Helen set a goal to complete her Master's degree within three years while managing her health condition and continuing to teach.

Challenges:

- Severe fatigue and physical limitations

- Balancing work, studies, and health management

- Emotional and mental stress from her condition

Strategies:

1. **Setting Realistic Goals:**

   - Helen broke her goal into smaller, manageable tasks. She set realistic timelines for completing coursework and allowed extra time for rest and recovery.

2. **Utilizing Support Systems:**

   - She leaned on her family, friends, and colleagues for emotional and practical support. Her school administration provided accommodations to help her manage her workload.

3. Seeking Professional Help:

- Helen worked closely with her medical team to manage her condition effectively. She also sought counseling to cope with the emotional stress.

4. Practicing Self-Care:

- She prioritized self-care by incorporating rest periods, maintaining a healthy diet, and engaging in gentle exercises to improve her energy levels.

5. Staying Organized:

- Helen used planners and digital tools to organize her schedule, track her progress, and ensure she met her deadlines.

6. Maintaining a Positive Mindset:

- She practiced positive affirmations and mindfulness techniques to stay focused and motivated. Helen reminded herself daily of her purpose and the impact she wanted to make through her work.

Results: Despite her health challenges, Helen successfully completed her Master's degree in three years. She continued to teach, inspiring her students and colleagues with her resilience and determination.

Lessons Learned:

- Setting realistic, achievable goals helps manage progress and prevent burnout.

- Leaning on support systems provides essential emotional and practical assistance.

- Seeking professional help for health and emotional well-being is crucial.

- Prioritizing self-care enhances overall resilience and energy levels.

- Staying organized ensures efficient management of multiple responsibilities.

- Maintaining a positive mindset and focusing on purpose drive motivation and perseverance.

Studies Supporting Helen's Success:

- Dr. Kelly McGonigal's research on stress management highlights the importance of positive stress responses and resilience-building practices.

- Dr. Barbara Fredrickson's broaden-and-build theory supports the benefits of positive emotions in enhancing well-being and resilience.

Story 2: Mark's Path to Entrepreneurship Amid Financial Struggles

Background: Mark, a 30-year-old software developer, faced significant financial struggles after losing his job during an economic downturn. Despite the challenges, he was determined to start his own tech company and create a stable future for himself and his family.

Goals: Mark aimed to launch his tech startup within a year and achieve financial stability within three years.

Challenges:

- Financial constraints and lack of initial capital

- High levels of stress and uncertainty

- Balancing personal responsibilities with entrepreneurial efforts

Strategies:

1. **Creating a Lean Startup Plan:**

   ○ Mark developed a lean startup plan that minimized initial expenses and focused on generating revenue quickly. He prioritized essential features and services to attract early customers.

2. **Leveraging Free Resources:**

○ He utilized free or low-cost resources, such as open-source software, online courses, and community support, to build his business. Mark also participated in local startup incubators and networking events.

3. Securing Small Funding:

○ Mark applied for small business grants and loans designed for startups. He also sought investment from family and friends to raise initial capital.

4. Building a Strong Support Network:

○ He connected with other entrepreneurs and mentors who provided guidance, advice, and moral support. Mark's network helped him navigate challenges and stay motivated.

5. Maintaining Financial Discipline:

○ Mark practiced strict financial discipline, tracking every expense and prioritizing investments that offered the highest returns. He avoided unnecessary expenses to ensure his startup remained viable.

6. Practicing Stress Management:

○ To manage stress, Mark incorporated regular exercise, meditation, and time with family into his routine. These practices helped him stay focused and maintain a positive outlook.

Results: Mark successfully launched his tech startup within a year and achieved financial stability within three years. His company grew steadily, and he was able to provide a stable income for his family. Mark's journey from financial struggles to entrepreneurial success became an inspiration to others in his community.

Lessons Learned:

- Creating a lean startup plan minimizes initial expenses and focuses on revenue generation.

- Leveraging free resources and community support can significantly reduce startup costs.

- Securing small funding from various sources provides the necessary capital to launch a business.

- Building a strong support network offers valuable guidance and motivation.

- Practicing financial discipline ensures the sustainability of the business.

- Incorporating stress management techniques enhances focus and resilience.

Studies Supporting Mark's Success:

- Dr. Saras Sarasvathy's effectuation theory emphasizes the

importance of leveraging available resources and partner-ships in entrepreneurship.

- Dr. Martin Seligman's research on positive psychology highlights the benefits of maintaining a positive outlook and practicing stress management for overall well-being and success.

Story 3: Lisa's Academic Achievement Despite Learning Disabilities

Background: Lisa, a 20-year-old college student, was diagnosed with dyslexia and ADHD, which made academic success particularly challenging. Despite these obstacles, Lisa was determined to graduate with honors and pursue a career in psychology.

Goals: Lisa aimed to graduate with honors within four years and gain admission to a prestigious graduate program in psychology.

Challenges:

- Learning disabilities that affected reading, writing, and concentration

- Managing time and maintaining focus on studies

- Overcoming self-doubt and societal stigma

Strategies:

1. **Utilizing Academic Support Services:**

   - Lisa accessed academic support services provided by her college, including tutoring, extended test time, and note-taking assistance. These resources helped her manage her coursework effectively.

2. **Developing Customized Study Techniques:**

- ○ She developed study techniques tailored to her learning style, such as using audiobooks, visual aids, and interactive learning tools. Lisa also practiced active learning methods to improve retention.

3. Time Management and Organization:

- ○ Lisa used planners and digital apps to organize her schedule, set reminders, and break down tasks into manageable steps. She prioritized her assignments and created a structured study routine.

4. Seeking Emotional Support:

- ○ She sought emotional support from family, friends, and counselors. This support network provided encouragement, understanding, and practical advice.

5. Building Self-Confidence:

- ○ Lisa focused on building her self-confidence through positive affirmations, setting small achievable goals, and celebrating her successes. She reminded herself of her strengths and potential.

6. Advocating for Herself:

- ○ Lisa actively communicated with her professors about her learning needs and advocated for necessary accommodations. This proactive approach ensured she received the support she needed.

Results: Lisa graduated with honors and was accepted into a prestigious graduate program in psychology. Her academic success, despite her learning disabilities, became a testament to her resilience, determination, and effective use of resources and support.

Lessons Learned:

- Utilizing academic support services provides essential assistance for managing coursework.

- Developing customized study techniques enhances learning and retention.

- Effective time management and organization improve productivity and reduce stress.

- Seeking emotional support from a network of family, friends, and counselors boosts motivation and resilience.

- Building self-confidence through positive affirmations and small goals reinforces belief in one's abilities.

- Advocating for oneself ensures necessary accommodations and support are received.

Studies Supporting Lisa's Success:

- Dr. Russell Barkley's research on ADHD and education emphasizes the importance of structured support and individualized learning strategies for academic success.

- Dr. G. Reid Lyon's studies on dyslexia highlight the benefits of tailored educational interventions and support services for students with learning disabilities.

Practical Applications and Studies

Implementing Resilience Techniques in Overcoming Adversity

1. **Health and Personal Challenges:**

    ○ **Setting Realistic Goals:** Break down larger goals into smaller, achievable tasks.

    ○ **Utilizing Support Systems:** Seek emotional and practical support from family, friends, and professionals.

    ○ **Practicing Self-Care:** Prioritize self-care practices to enhance overall well-being.

    ○ **Staying Organized:** Use planners and digital tools to manage time and tasks effectively.

    ○ **Maintaining a Positive Mindset:** Practice positive affirmations and mindfulness techniques.

2. Financial and Entrepreneurial Challenges:

- **Creating a Lean Startup Plan:** Develop a plan that minimizes expenses and focuses on revenue generation.

- **Leveraging Free Resources:** Utilize free or low-cost resources to build and grow the business.

- **Securing Small Funding:** Explore various funding options to raise initial capital.

- **Building a Support Network:** Connect with other entrepreneurs and mentors for guidance and support.

- **Practicing Stress Management:** Incorporate stress management techniques to maintain focus and resilience.

3. Academic and Learning Challenges:

- **Utilizing Academic Support Services:** Access available support services to manage coursework effectively.

- **Developing Customized Study Techniques:** Tailor study techniques to suit individual learning styles.

- **Time Management and Organization:** Implement time management strategies and organizational tools.

- **Seeking Emotional Support:** Build a support network for encouragement and understanding.

- **Building Self-Confidence:** Focus on strengths, set small goals, and celebrate successes.

- **Advocating for Oneself:** Communicate needs and seek necessary accommodations and support.

Scientific Studies Supporting Resilience:

1. Study by Dr. Kelly McGonigal:

- Dr. McGonigal's research on stress management highlights the benefits of positive stress responses and resilience-building practices. Her findings emphasize the importance of viewing stress as a challenge rather than a threat.

2. Study by Dr. Martin Seligman:

- Dr. Seligman's research on positive psychology demonstrates that maintaining a positive outlook and practicing resilience techniques enhance overall well-being and success. His studies support the value of positive thinking and stress management.

3. Study by Dr. Russell Barkley:

- Dr. Barkley's research on ADHD and education emphasizes the importance of structured support and individualized learning strategies for students with learning disabilities. His findings highlight the benefits of tailored educational interventions.

4. **Study by Dr. Barbara Fredrickson:**

- Dr. Fredrickson's broaden-and-build theory supports the benefits of positive emotions in enhancing well-being and resilience. Her research shows that positive emotions help build personal resources and improve overall life satisfaction.

Conclusion

In this chapter, we've explored inspiring stories of individuals who overcame significant adversity to achieve their goals. These stories highlight the importance of resilience, effective goal-setting, and the support of networks and resources. By understanding their strategies and drawing from scientific research, you can apply similar techniques to overcome your own challenges.

Remember that overcoming adversity requires setting realistic goals, utilizing support systems, practicing self-care, and maintaining a positive mindset. Whether facing health challenges, financial struggles, or learning disabilities, resilience and determination can lead to remarkable achievements.

As we continue our journey, let these stories of resilience inspire and empower you to stay focused and motivated. Together, we can overcome obstacles and achieve greatness through perseverance and effective goal-setting.

Stay resilient, stay focused, and let's achieve our goals despite adversity.

16

UNCONVENTIONAL PATHS TO SUCCESS

In the previous chapter, we delved into stories of resilience and the techniques used by individuals to overcome significant adversity. Now, let's explore the fascinating world of unconventional paths to success. This chapter will highlight unique success stories that defy traditional expectations and provide valuable insights and lessons from these extraordinary journeys. These stories demonstrate that success is not always linear and that unconventional approaches can lead to remarkable achievements.

Unique Success Stories

Story 1: The Rise of a YouTube Sensation

Background: Laura, a 25-year-old aspiring musician, struggled to break into the highly competitive music industry. Despite her talent and passion, traditional routes like getting signed by a record label seemed out of reach. Laura decided to take an unconventional path by leveraging the power of the internet.

Goals: Laura aimed to build a loyal audience for her music and establish a sustainable career as an independent artist.

Challenges:

- Limited financial resources for professional recording and promotion

- High competition and oversaturation in the online music space

- Balancing content creation with other responsibilities

Strategies:

1. **Utilizing Social Media Platforms:**

   ○ Laura created a YouTube channel where she posted covers of popular songs, original compositions, and behind-the-scenes content. She also used platforms like Instagram and Twitter to engage with her audience and promote her videos.

2. **Consistent Content Creation:**

○ She committed to a regular posting schedule, uploading new videos every week. Consistency helped her build a loyal following and improve her skills over time.

3. Engaging with the Audience:

○ Laura actively engaged with her audience by responding to comments, taking song requests, and hosting live Q&A sessions. This interaction fostered a strong community and increased her visibility.

4. Collaborations:

○ She collaborated with other YouTube musicians and influencers to reach new audiences. These collaborations introduced her to a wider fan base and provided valuable networking opportunities.

5. Monetization:

○ Laura monetized her channel through ad revenue, sponsorships, and fan donations via platforms like Patreon. She also sold merchandise and offered exclusive content to her supporters.

6. Adapting and Innovating:

○ Laura stayed adaptable by experimenting with different video formats and content styles. She kept up with trends and continuously sought ways to innovate and stand out.

Results: Laura's YouTube channel grew rapidly, amassing millions of subscribers and views. Her unique blend of talent, consistency, and audience engagement turned her into a YouTube sensation. She eventually released her own albums independently and embarked on successful tours, achieving her dream of a sustainable music career.

Lessons Learned:

- Leveraging social media platforms provides access to a global audience and opportunities for independent success.

- Consistent content creation builds a loyal following and improves skills over time.

- Active engagement with the audience fosters a strong community and increases visibility.

- Collaborations expand reach and provide valuable networking opportunities.

- Monetization through multiple streams creates financial stability.

- Staying adaptable and innovative helps maintain relevance and stand out in a crowded space.

Studies Supporting Laura's Success:

- Dr. Jonah Berger's research on social influence and viral marketing highlights the importance of social media engagement and content virality.

- Dr. Henry Jenkins' studies on participatory culture emphasize the value of audience interaction and community building in the digital age.

Story 2: The Entrepreneur Who Revolutionized an Industry

Background: Sam, a 35-year-old engineer, noticed inefficiencies and a lack of innovation in the traditional manufacturing industry. He was passionate about sustainability and wanted to create a business that addressed these issues. Instead of following conventional business practices, Sam decided to revolutionize the industry with a novel approach.

Goals: Sam aimed to create a sustainable manufacturing company that utilized cutting-edge technology and eco-friendly practices.

Challenges:

- High initial costs and investment for innovative technology

- Resistance from established industry players

- Need for specialized knowledge and expertise

Strategies:

1. Embracing Technology:

- Sam invested in advanced manufacturing technologies like 3D printing, automation, and AI-driven quality control. These technologies improved efficiency, reduced waste, and minimized environmental impact.

2. Sustainable Practices:

○ He implemented eco-friendly practices, such as using renewable energy sources, recycling materials, and designing products for longevity and recyclability. Sustainability was a core value of his business.

3. Crowdfunding and Grants:

○ To overcome financial challenges, Sam utilized crowdfunding platforms to raise initial capital. He also applied for grants focused on innovation and sustainability.

4. Building a Specialized Team:

○ Sam recruited experts in technology, sustainability, and manufacturing to build a knowledgeable and innovative team. Their expertise drove the company's success and continuous improvement.

5. Creating Strategic Partnerships:

○ He formed partnerships with other innovative companies and research institutions. These collaborations provided access to new technologies, shared knowledge, and opened up new markets.

6. Educating and Influencing:

○ Sam actively promoted the benefits of sustainable manufacturing through industry conferences, publications, and social media. He aimed to educate and influence others in the industry to adopt similar practices.

Results: Sam's company quickly gained recognition for its innovative and sustainable approach. It became a leader in the industry, attracting clients who valued efficiency and environmental responsibility. The company's success demonstrated that unconventional approaches could drive significant change and profitability in traditional industries.

Lessons Learned:

- Embracing advanced technology can drive efficiency and innovation.

- Implementing sustainable practices attracts environmentally conscious clients and reduces long-term costs.

- Crowdfunding and grants provide valuable funding sources for innovative projects.

- Building a specialized team ensures expertise and continuous improvement.

- Strategic partnerships expand resources and market opportunities.

- Educating and influencing others fosters industry-wide change.

Studies Supporting Sam's Success:

- Dr. Clayton Christensen's theory of disruptive innovation highlights how new technologies and business models can revolutionize industries.

- Dr. Michael Porter's research on competitive strategy emphasizes the importance of sustainability as a strategic advantage in modern business.

Story 3: The Career Changer Who Found Success in a New Field

Background: Anna, a 40-year-old corporate lawyer, felt unfulfilled in her career and wanted to pursue her passion for culinary arts. Despite having no formal training in the field, Anna decided to make a bold career change and follow her dream of becoming a chef and opening her own restaurant.

Goals: Anna aimed to complete a culinary arts program, gain experience in the industry, and open her own restaurant within five years.

Challenges:

- Lack of formal training and experience in the culinary field

- Financial risks associated with career change and starting a business

- Overcoming self-doubt and societal expectations

Strategies:

1. **Pursuing Education:**

    ◦ Anna enrolled in a reputable culinary arts program to gain the necessary skills and knowledge. She balanced her studies with part-time work to manage her finances.

2. Gaining Experience:

- ◦ She sought internships and entry-level positions in various kitchens to gain hands-on experience and learn from established chefs. This experience was invaluable in honing her skills and understanding the industry.

3. Building a Personal Brand:

- ◦ Anna started a food blog and social media accounts to document her culinary journey. She shared recipes, cooking tips, and behind-the-scenes insights, building a following and establishing her brand.

4. Networking:

- ◦ She attended culinary events, workshops, and industry conferences to network with professionals and gain insights. Anna's networking efforts helped her build valuable connections and mentorships.

5. Developing a Business Plan:

- ◦ Anna created a detailed business plan for her restaurant, including market research, financial projections, and a unique value proposition. This plan guided her steps and helped secure funding.

6. Seeking Investors and Partners:

○ She presented her business plan to potential investors and partners, securing the necessary funding to start her restaurant. Anna's passion and thorough planning impressed her backers.

Results: Within five years, Anna successfully transitioned from a corporate lawyer to a renowned chef and restaurant owner. Her restaurant became a local favorite, known for its innovative dishes and warm atmosphere. Anna's journey inspired others to pursue their passions, regardless of age or background.

Lessons Learned:

- Pursuing education and gaining relevant experience are crucial for career change.

- Building a personal brand enhances visibility and establishes credibility.

- Networking provides valuable connections, mentorship, and industry insights.

- Developing a detailed business plan guides steps and helps secure funding.

- Seeking investors and partners can provide necessary financial support.

- Overcoming self-doubt and societal expectations is essential for following one's passion.

Studies Supporting Anna's Success:

- Dr. Herminia Ibarra's research on career transitions highlights the importance of experimenting with new roles and building a personal brand during career changes.

- Dr. Daniel Goleman's studies on emotional intelligence emphasize the role of self-awareness and resilience in successfully navigating career transitions.

Practical Applications and Studies

Implementing Unconventional Success Strategies in Your Goals

1. **Leveraging Technology and Social Media:**

   - Utilize social media platforms and digital tools to reach a global audience and build a personal or business brand.

   - Stay consistent with content creation and engage actively with your audience to foster a strong community.

2. **Embracing Innovation and Sustainability:**

   - Invest in advanced technologies and sustainable practices to drive efficiency and attract conscious consumers.

○ Form strategic partnerships and leverage available resources to overcome financial and operational challenges.

3. Pursuing Passion and Career Change:

○ Seek education and gain relevant experience to transition into a new field.

○ Build a personal brand and network actively to establish credibility and gain support.

○ Develop a detailed business plan and seek investors or partners to support your venture.

Scientific Studies Supporting Unconventional Paths:

1. Study by Dr. Jonah Berger:

○ Dr. Berger's research on social influence and viral marketing underscores the importance of social media engagement and content virality in achieving success in unconventional ways.

2. Study by Dr. Clayton Christensen:

○ Dr. Christensen's theory of disruptive innovation highlights how new technologies and business models can revolutionize industries and create new opportunities for success.

3. Study by Dr. Herminia Ibarra:

- Dr. Ibarra's research on career transitions emphasizes the importance of experimenting with new roles, building a personal brand, and leveraging networks during career changes.

4. Study by Dr. Daniel Goleman:

- Dr. Goleman's studies on emotional intelligence demonstrate the role of self-awareness, resilience, and adaptability in successfully navigating unconventional paths to success.

Conclusion

In this chapter, we've explored inspiring stories of individuals who achieved success through unconventional paths. These stories highlight the importance of leveraging technology, embracing innovation, pursuing passion, and building strong networks. By understanding their unique strategies and drawing from scientific research, you can apply similar techniques to achieve your own goals.

Remember that success is not always linear, and unconventional approaches can lead to remarkable achievements. Stay open to new possibilities, embrace innovation, and pursue your passions with determination and resilience. Let these unique success stories inspire and empower you to carve your own path to success.

Stay innovative, stay passionate, and let's achieve our goals through unconventional paths.

17

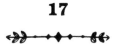

KEY POINTS

As we reach the conclusion of this book, it's time to recap the key points we've covered and provide you with a final burst of motivation. Throughout these chapters, we've explored a multitude of strategies, techniques, and inspirational stories aimed at helping you set, pursue, and achieve your goals. Whether you're aiming for personal growth, professional advancement, or overcoming adversity, the lessons in this book are designed to guide you on your journey.

Recap of Key Points

Chapter 1: What Are Goals?

- We defined goals and differentiated them from dreams.

- We explored different types of goals: short-term, medium-term, and long-term.

- Emphasized the importance of setting clear, actionable goals for personal and professional growth.

Chapter 2: The Science Behind Goal Setting

- Discussed how goal setting impacts the brain, including motivation and reward systems.

- Highlighted the neurological insights related to goal setting, such as neuroplasticity and habit formation.

- Explored the benefits of goal setting, including increased focus, productivity, and self-esteem.

Chapter 3: Common Myths About Goal Setting

- Debunked common misconceptions about goal setting.

- Examined why some people fail to achieve their goals due to lack of planning, commitment, and relying solely on external motivation.

- Provided real-life examples to illustrate goal-setting failures and successes.

Chapter 4: The SMART Method

- Introduced the SMART criteria for setting goals: Specific,

Measurable, Achievable, Relevant, Time-bound.

- Provided a detailed breakdown of each component with examples in various areas like health, career, and personal growth.

Chapter 5: Other Goal-Setting Frameworks

- Explored alternative frameworks such as OKRs (Objectives and Key Results), BHAGs (Big Hairy Audacious Goals), and WOOP (Wish, Outcome, Obstacle, Plan).

- Discussed the benefits and practical applications of these frameworks.

Chapter 6: Vision Boards and Visualization

- Examined the power of visualization and its psychological benefits.

- Provided techniques for effective visualization and a step-by-step guide to creating vision boards.

- Shared success stories of individuals who achieved their goals through visualization.

Chapter 7: Writing Down Your Goals

- Highlighted the psychological benefits of writing down goals.

- Discussed journaling techniques and digital tools for goal tracking.

- Provided practical tips for effective goal documentation.

Chapter 8: Creating Action Plans

- Emphasized the importance of breaking down goals into actionable steps.

- Discussed techniques for prioritizing tasks, such as the Eisenhower Matrix and the Pareto Principle.

- Explained how to set realistic deadlines and monitor progress.

Chapter 9: Overcoming Obstacles

- Identified common obstacles in goal achievement and techniques to maintain motivation.

- Shared resilience stories of individuals overcoming adversity.

- Discussed practical applications and scientific studies supporting resilience techniques.

Chapter 10: Time Management and Productivity

- Explored effective time management strategies like the Pomodoro Technique and time blocking.

- Provided productivity hacks to increase efficiency and manage multiple goals simultaneously.

- Discussed the importance of balancing goals and regular progress reviews.

Chapter 11: Accountability and Support Systems

- Highlighted the role of accountability partners and building a support network.

- Discussed the benefits of joining goal-setting groups and communities.

- Provided practical advice on finding and maintaining support systems.

Chapter 12: Reviewing and Adjusting Goals

- Emphasized the importance of regular goal reviews and adapting goals based on progress.

- Discussed techniques for effective reviews and the significance of celebrating milestones.

- Shared practical applications and studies supporting regular goal adjustments.

Chapter 13: Personal Goals Achieved

- Presented inspirational stories of individuals achieving

personal goals.

- Provided key takeaways and practical advice from their journeys.

- Discussed scientific studies supporting the strategies used in these success stories.

Chapter 14: Professional Goals Achieved

- Highlighted examples of professional goal achievement in career and business.

- Provided lessons and strategies from successful individuals.

- Discussed scientific studies supporting professional success strategies.

Chapter 15: Overcoming Adversity

- Shared stories of individuals overcoming significant obstacles to achieve their goals.

- Discussed techniques used to stay focused and motivated despite challenges.

- Provided practical applications and scientific studies supporting resilience.

Chapter 16: Unconventional Paths to Success

- Presented unique success stories of individuals achieving goals through unconventional paths.

- Provided insights and lessons from these unique journeys.

- Discussed scientific studies supporting unconventional success strategies.

Encouragement

Throughout this book, we have seen that the journey to achieving goals is rarely straightforward. It is filled with challenges, setbacks, and moments of self-doubt. However, it is also a journey of growth, discovery, and transformation. The stories and strategies shared here are meant to inspire and equip you with the tools you need to navigate your own path.

Remember, success is not defined by how quickly you reach your goals but by the persistence and resilience you show along the way. Every step you take, no matter how small, brings you closer to your dreams. Celebrate your progress, learn from your setbacks, and never lose sight of your vision.

The road to success is paved with determination, adaptability, and a willingness to learn. Embrace the process, stay committed to your goals, and believe in your ability to achieve greatness.

Call to Action

Now, it's time to take the first step on your goal-setting journey. Here's how you can start:

1. **Reflect on Your Goals:**

   ○ Take some time to reflect on what you truly want to achieve. Consider your passions, values, and long-term vision.

2. **Set Clear, Actionable Goals:**

   ○ Use the SMART criteria or any other goal-setting framework that resonates with you. Write down your goals and break them into actionable steps.

3. **Create an Action Plan:**

   ○ Develop a detailed action plan outlining the steps needed to achieve your goals. Set deadlines and prioritize tasks to stay organized and focused.

4. **Find Accountability Partners:**

   ○ Connect with friends, family, or colleagues who can support and motivate you. Share your goals with them and establish regular check-ins.

5. **Join Supportive Communities:**

○ Seek out groups and communities that share your interests and goals. Engage actively and draw inspiration and support from others.

6. **Regularly Review and Adjust:**

○ Schedule regular reviews to assess your progress and make necessary adjustments. Stay flexible and adapt your plans as needed.

7. **Celebrate Your Achievements:**

○ Recognize and celebrate your milestones. Reward yourself for your hard work and dedication.

8. **Stay Motivated and Resilient:**

○ Use the techniques discussed in this book to maintain motivation and overcome obstacles. Remember, resilience is key to achieving long-term success.

9. **Keep Learning and Growing:**

○ Continuously seek new knowledge, skills, and experiences. Embrace challenges as opportunities for growth.

Your journey begins now. The path to achieving your goals is filled with possibilities, and you have the power to shape your future.

Stay focused, stay motivated, and let the lessons and stories in this book guide you toward success.

Together, we can achieve greatness.

Final Motivational Message

As you embark on your goal-setting journey, remember that you are capable of achieving remarkable things. The potential within you is limitless, and with the right mindset, strategies, and support, you can turn your dreams into reality.

Stay committed to your goals, believe in yourself, and never give up. The journey may be challenging, but the rewards are worth it. Embrace the process, celebrate your progress, and keep moving forward with determination and resilience.

You have the power to create the life you envision. Start today, take that first step, and watch as your efforts transform your dreams into reality. The future is yours to shape, and success is within your reach.

Stay inspired, stay motivated, and let's achieve our goals together.

Thank you for joining me on this journey. Here's to your success and the incredible achievements that lie ahead.

APPENDICES

In the previous chapters, we have covered extensive strategies, inspiring stories, and practical advice on setting and achieving goals. To help you put these lessons into action, this section provides additional resources, including goal-setting templates, recommended reading, and notes and references. These tools will support you in your journey towards success and provide further insights into effective goal-setting and achievement.

Goal-Setting Templates

To make your goal-setting process more organized and actionable, we have included a variety of templates and worksheets. These templates are designed to help you articulate your goals, break them into manageable steps, and track your progress effectively.

Template 1: SMART Goals Worksheet

Use this worksheet to define your goals according to the SMART criteria—Specific, Measurable, Achievable, Relevant, Time-bound.

Goal	Specific (What do you want to achieve?)	Measurable (How will you track progress?)	Achievable (Is it realistic?)	Relevant (Why is it important?)	Time-bound (What is the deadline?)
Example: Improve Fitness	Lose 10 pounds in 3 months	Weekly weigh-ins and fitness tracking app	Yes, with a balanced diet and exercise	To improve health and well-being	3 months from start date

Template 2: Action Plan Template

This template helps you break down your goals into specific actions, set deadlines, and assign priorities.

Goal	Action Steps	Deadline	Priority	Progress	Notes
Example: Write a Book	Complete outline	March 1st	High	50%	Need to finalize chapter topics
	Write first draft	June 1st	High	20%	Allocate more time on weekends
	Revise and edit	August 1st	Medium	0%	Seek feedback from beta readers

Template 3: Weekly Review Template

Use this template to conduct regular reviews of your progress, identify challenges, and adjust your plans.

Week	Goals	Achievements	Challenges	Adjustments Needed	Notes
Example: Week 1	Complete Chapter 1	Finished draft of Chapter 1	Time management issues	Allocate more writing time	Celebrate with a movie night

Template 4: Vision Board Template

This template provides a structured approach to creating a vision board that aligns with your goals.

Category	Images and Words	Description	Deadline	Progress	Notes
Example: Career	Pictures of successful entrepreneurs, words like "innovation" and "leadership"	Represents my goal to start a business	December 31st	30%	Add quotes from role models

Template 5: Goal Tracking Journal

This journal template helps you document your daily progress, reflect on your achievements, and stay motivated.

Date	Goal	Today's Actions	Achievements	Challenges	Reflections
Example: Jan 1	Improve Fitness	30-minute run, healthy meals	Completed run, ate healthy all day	Felt tired in the evening	Need to rest more at night

Recommended Reading

For those who want to delve deeper into the world of goal-setting, motivation, and personal development, here are some highly recommended books and resources:

1. **"Atomic Habits" by James Clear:**

   - A comprehensive guide on how small changes can lead to remarkable results. Clear provides actionable strategies for building good habits and breaking bad ones.

2. **"Grit: The Power of Passion and Perseverance" by Angela Duckworth:**

   - Duckworth's research-based insights into the importance of grit and how perseverance and passion contribute to success.

3. **"The Power of Habit" by Charles Duhigg:**

   - An exploration of the science behind habits and how understanding them can lead to personal and professional growth.

4. **"Mindset: The New Psychology of Success" by Carol S. Dweck:**

○ Dweck's groundbreaking work on fixed and growth mindsets and how adopting a growth mindset can lead to greater achievement.

5. **"Drive: The Surprising Truth About What Motivates Us" by Daniel H. Pink:**

○ An in-depth look at the factors that truly motivate us and how to harness them to achieve our goals.

6. **"The 7 Habits of Highly Effective People" by Stephen R. Covey:**

○ Covey's timeless principles for personal and professional effectiveness.

7. **"The Lean Startup" by Eric Ries:**

○ A guide for entrepreneurs on how to build and grow successful startups through innovation and adaptability.

8. **"Getting Things Done: The Art of Stress-Free Productivity" by David Allen:**

○ Allen's methodology for staying organized and productive in a busy world.

9. **"The Compound Effect" by Darren Hardy:**

○ How small, consistent actions can lead to significant results over time.

10. "The Four Tendencies" by Gretchen Rubin:

○ Rubin's framework for understanding how different personality types respond to expectations and how this knowledge can improve goal-setting and achievement.

Notes and References

Throughout this book, we have referenced numerous studies, theories, and expert insights to provide a solid foundation for the strategies and advice shared. Here is a compilation of the key references and additional resources for further exploration:

1. **Study by Dr. Gail Matthews:**

   ○ Matthews, G. (2007). "The Impact of Commitment, Accountability, and Written Goals on Goal Achievement." Dominican University of California.

2. **Research by Dr. Kelly McGonigal:**

   ○ McGonigal, K. (2015). "The Upside of Stress: Why Stress Is Good for You, and How to Get Good at It." Avery Publishing.

3. **Broaden-and-Build Theory by Dr. Barbara Fredrickson:**

   ○ Fredrickson, B. L. (2001). "The Role of Positive Emotions in Positive Psychology: The Broaden-and-Build Theory of Positive Emotions." American Psychologist, 56(3), 218-226.

4. **Grit Research by Dr. Angela Duckworth:**

   ○ Duckworth, A. L., & Quinn, P. D. (2009). "Development and Validation of the Short Grit Scale (Grit-S)." Journal of Personality Assessment, 91(2), 166-174.

5. Growth Mindset Theory by Dr. Carol Dweck:

- Dweck, C. S. (2006). "Mindset: The New Psychology of Success." Random House.

6. Effectuation Theory by Dr. Saras Sarasvathy:

- Sarasvathy, S. D. (2001). "Causation and Effectuation: Toward a Theoretical Shift from Economic Inevitability to Entrepreneurial Contingency." Academy of Management Review, 26(2), 243-263.

7. Disruptive Innovation by Dr. Clayton Christensen:

- Christensen, C. M. (1997). "The Innovator's Dilemma: When New Technologies Cause Great Firms to Fail." Harvard Business Review Press.

8. Social Influence Research by Dr. Jonah Berger:

- Berger, J. (2013). "Contagious: How to Build Word of Mouth in the Digital Age." Simon & Schuster.

9. Participatory Culture by Dr. Henry Jenkins:

- Jenkins, H. (2009). "Confronting the Challenges of Participatory Culture: Media Education for the 21st

Century." MIT Press.

10. **Career Transitions by Dr. Herminia Ibarra:**

- Ibarra, H. (2003). "Working Identity: Unconventional Strategies for Reinventing Your Career." Harvard Business Review Press.

11. **Emotional Intelligence by Dr. Daniel Goleman:**

- Goleman, D. (1995). "Emotional Intelligence: Why It Can Matter More Than IQ." Bantam Books.

Final Thoughts

As you embark on your goal-setting journey, use these templates, recommended readings, and references as tools to guide and support you. The knowledge and strategies shared in this book, combined with your determination and resilience, will help you achieve your aspirations.

Remember, the path to success is unique for everyone. Embrace the process, learn from each step, and celebrate your progress. The journey is just as important as the destination, and every challenge you overcome makes you stronger and more capable.

Stay inspired, stay focused, and let's achieve greatness together.

Thank you for joining me on this journey. Here's to your success and the incredible achievements that lie ahead.

This concludes our comprehensive guide on goal-setting and achievement. Keep this book as a reference and continue to apply the lessons and strategies as you pursue your goals. Success is within your reach—take the first step today and never look back.